PREDICTING PRESIDENTIAL ELECTIONS
AND OTHER THINGS

PREDICTING

PRESIDENTIAL ELECTIONS

AND OTHER THINGS

Ray C. Fair

STANFORD BUSINESS BOOKS
An Imprint of Stanford University Press

Stanford University Press
Stanford, California
©2002 by the Board of Trustees
of the Leland Stanford Junior University

Printed in the United States of America on acid-free, archival-quality paper.

Library of Congress Cataloging-in-Publication Data

Fair, Ray C.
Predicting presidential elections and other things /
Ray C. Fair
   p. cm.
  Includes bibliographical references and index.
  ISBN 0-8047-4509-9 (alk. paper)
   1. Social prediction. 2. Presidents--United States--Election--Forecasting.
3.Election Forecasting--United States. 4. Economic forecasting.
  HM901 .F35 2002
  303.4973 21

                                           2002021186
Original Printing 2002

Last figure below indicates year of this printing:
11   10   09   08   07   06   05   04   03   02

Designed by Rob Ehle.
Typeset by Interactive Composition Corporation in 10/13.5 Sabon.

Contents

Acknowledgments

My greatest debt is to my wife, Sharon Oster, and my children, Emily Fair Oster, Stephen Oster Fair, and John Fair Oster. Over the course of many years they have provided numerous useful suggestions and complaints. They have talked me out of such titles as "What Can Econometricians Do?" and "Econometrics Made Easy." They have read many drafts and tried to keep me focused when I got carried away explaining some technique.

I am also indebted to Terry Seaks, who read the manuscript from cover to cover with many useful comments. Terry saved me from numerous errors. Jennifer Nou provided valuable research assistance. Others who read parts of the manuscript and provided helpful comments include Orley Ashenfelter, John Covell, Fred Djang, John Ferejohn, and Andrew Leigh.

Last but not least I am indebted to Ken MacLeod for much advice and encouragement. Without Ken's support I am not sure this book would ever have been completed.

PREDICTING PRESIDENTIAL ELECTIONS
AND OTHER THINGS

Introduction
What This Book Is About

If you have glanced at the table of contents, you might be wondering what the topics in this book could possibly have in common. They include presidential elections, extramarital affairs, wine quality, college grades, marathon times, interest rates, and inflation. The answer is that they can all be explained and analyzed using the tools of the social sciences and statistics. The aim of this book is to allow those who are not necessarily well versed in these tools to see how this is done. The widely differing topics have been chosen to show the broad range of these tools and their strengths and weaknesses.

This book does not require that you be a social scientist or statistician or even that you like them. It is also fine if you don't know a Greek letter from a happy face symbol. The book simply requires some patience in following the movement from a general idea of how something works to a specific prediction of what it will be in the future. The steps involved in this process can be explained without resort to technical material. By the end of the book you should have a deeper understanding not only of the particular topics discussed but also of the way topics like these can be analyzed.

Knowledge of social science procedures allows a more critical reading of opinions and predictions that we are bombarded with every day. Is there any support for a particular opinion? How might the opinion be tested? How much confidence can we place in the prediction? The problem of evaluating views is harder than ever now that we are in the Internet age. Information is available at the click of a mouse, and views can be backed up by vast amounts of information. But is the information any good?

Consider, for example, the topic of U.S. presidential elections. What factors are important in deciding who will win an election? There are many views. Some stress the personalities of the candidates, others stress the amount of money available to the campaigns, still others stress the economy, and so on. Although each view has a story with it, the problem is that there are too many stories. How do we separate the wheat from the chaff? We need some way of deciding which stories have something to them and which do not. One way comprises tools of the social sciences and statistics, which this book discusses. We will see that past election results can be used in a systematic way to decide which stories appear to have merit. But we can do more than this. We can also use the information from past elections to *predict* the outcome of an election that has not yet taken place. We can both explain, in terms of telling a story that seems consistent with past results, and predict.

So what are these mysterious tools? We begin with some question of interest, such as what determines the outcomes of presidential elections. Why did Richard Nixon beat George McGovern in 1972, and why did Ronald Reagan beat Jimmy Carter in 1980? We usually have some initial ideas about the answer to our question. The economy may play an important role in influencing how people vote, so an obvious initial idea is that the economy affects voting behavior. Another obvious initial idea is that an incumbent president running again may have an advantage because he can use the powers of the presidency to try to sway votes.

We call an idea or a set of ideas offered to explain something a *theory*. A theory may or may not be a good explanation. For example, a theory that says that people vote for a candidate solely on the basis of his or her height is not likely to be a good explanation of the way people actually vote. A theory need not be original with you, and it does not really matter where it came from. What is important is that there be some way to test whether the theory is any good.

How would one test the theory that the economy affects voting behavior? This is where past election results come into play. We can collect data on the economy and on past election outcomes and see how closely the theory explains the data. Was it generally the case that the incumbent party won when the economy was good and lost when the economy was bad? This movement from proposing a theory to testing the theory using data is what much of this book is about. We will see that an important feature about testing theories is that once the tests have been performed it is usually possible to move fairly easily to prediction.

The topics in this book have been chosen to appeal to a wide range of people. Political junkies and others interested in voting behavior should find the results on presidential elections helpful in understanding how people vote. Other dimensions of human behavior are covered in the chapters on extramarital affairs and college grades. In the chapter on extramarital affairs we examine the factors that increase or decrease the chances that someone will have an affair. In the chapter on college grades we examine how class attendance affects grades. As those of us who teach college students know, not every student shows up for every class. Does this matter in terms of grades, and if so, how much?

The chapter on wine quality shows that the quality that a new wine eventually achieves after proper aging can be predicted fairly well by simply knowing what the weather was like in the harvest year. This knowledge can help one decide whether a new wine is under- or over-priced and thus whether one should purchase it.

More serious investment issues are the concern of the chapters on interest rates and inflation. These chapters discuss how interest rates and inflation can be explained and predicted.

The chapter on marathon times should be of special interest to people over age 35. It gives estimates of how fast people slow down as they age. If you are a runner over 35 and have noticed that you are not quite as fast as you used to be, you can see if you are slowing down faster than you should be. The nice thing about this chapter is that it shows that you need not feel bad just because you are slowing down. You only need feel bad if you are slowing down too fast!

This book may also appeal to college students taking introductory courses in the social sciences and statistics. It provides an intuitive discussion of the tools used in these courses and contains a number of examples of their use. It is often said that the three main interests of college students are sex, drinking, and sports, with perhaps grades ranked fourth. This book has all four!

The most difficult chapter in the book is Chapter 2, which discusses the tools. The chapter is divided into seven lessons, one for each day of the week. Lesson 4 on Thursday is the hardest. It explains a key test statistic, the *t-statistic*, showing why a *t*-statistic that is greater than about 2 is supportive of the theory being tested, whereas a smaller value is not. If you are willing to take this result—that large *t*-statistics are supportive of a theory and small ones are not—on faith, you may skip Lesson 4. You will miss an explanation of why this is true, but this should not hinder your reading the rest of the book. Also, if the material in Chapter 2 is completely new to you, you may want to read the chapter quickly the first time through and then come back to it as you go through the examples in Chapters 3 and beyond.

The tools in Chapter 2 are best explained using an example, and we will use voting behavior in presidential elections as the example. Chapter 1 introduces this topic. It presents a theory of what determines votes for president and discusses the data that are available to test the theory. This sets the stage for Chapter 2, which explains the tools. Chapters 3 and 4 continue the discussion of presidential elections using the tools from Chapter 2. Each of the remaining chapters is a separate topic, each using the tools from Chapter 2. These chapters need not be read in order, although Chapter 9 on interest rates should be read before Chapter 10 on inflation. The Chapter Notes at the end of the book gives references.

In his advice to Harvard students in *Under Which Lyre,* W. H. Auden wrote:

> Thou shalt not answer questionnaires
> Or quizzes upon World-Affairs,
>   Nor with compliance
> Take any test. Thou shalt not sit
> With statisticians nor commit
>   A social science.

Alas, I am giving the opposite advice. Come sit with statisticians and social scientists for a while and see what they can do.

1   It's the Economy, Stupid

Election night at midnight:
Boy Bryan's defeat.
Defeat of western silver.
Defeat of the wheat.
Victory of letterfiles
And plutocrats in miles
With dollar signs upon their coats,
Diamond watchchains on their vests and spats on their feet.

Vachel Lindsay, from Bryan, Bryan, Bryan, Bryan

A common pastime in the United States every four years is predicting presidential elections. Polls are taken almost daily in the year of an election, and there are now Web sites that allow betting on elections.

Some of the more interesting footnotes to presidential elections concern large errors that were made in predicting who would win. In 1936 the *Literary Digest* predicted a victory for Republican Alfred Landon over Democrat Franklin Roosevelt by a fairly large margin, when in fact Roosevelt won election to a second term by a landslide. The *Literary Digest* polled more than two million people, so the sample size was huge, but the sample was selected from telephone directories and automobile registrations, which overrepresented wealthy and urban voters, more of whom supported Landon. In addition, the response rate was higher for voters who supported Landon. The *Literary Digest* never really recovered from this error, and it ceased publication in 1938.

Another famous error was made by the *Chicago Tribune* in 1948, when it ran the headline "Dewey Wins." After it became clear that Thomas Dewey had lost, a smiling Harry Truman was photographed holding up the headline.

A more recent large error was made in June 1988, when most polls were predicting that Michael Dukakis would beat George Bush by about 17 percentage points. A few weeks later the polls began predicting a Bush victory, which turned out to be correct.

While interesting in their own right, polls are limited in helping us understand what motivates people to vote the way they do. Most polls simply ask people their voting plans, not how or why they arrived at these plans. We must go beyond simple polling results to learn about the factors that influence voting behavior, which is where tools of the social sciences and statistics can be of help.

A Theory of Voting Behavior

To examine the question of why people vote the way they do, we begin with a theory. Consider a person entering a voting booth and deciding which lever to pull for president. Some people are dyed-in-the-wool Republicans and always vote for the Republican candidate. Conversely, some are dyed-in-the-wool Democrats and always vote Democratic. For others, one issue, such as abortion or gun control, dominates all others, and they always vote for the candidate on their side of the issue. For these people there is not much to explain. One could try to explain why someone became a staunch Republican or Democrat or was focused on only one issue, but this is not the main concern here. Of concern here are all the other voters, whom we will call *swing voters*. Swing voters are those without strong ideological ties whose views about which party to vote for may change from election to election. For example, Missouri is considered a swing state (that is, a state with many swing voters). It sometimes votes Democratic and sometimes Republican. Massachusetts, on the other hand, almost always votes Democratic, regardless of the state of the economy or anything else, and Idaho almost always votes Republican. The percentage of swing voters in these two states is much smaller than the percentage in Missouri.

What do swing voters think about when they enter the booth? One theory is that swing voters think about how well off financially they expect to be in the future under each candidate and vote for the candidate under whom they expect to be better off. If they expect that their financial situation will be better off under the Democratic candidate, they vote for him or her; otherwise they vote for the Republican candidate. This is the theory that people "vote their pocketbooks." The theory need not pertain to all voters, but for it to be of quantitative interest it must pertain to a fairly large number.

The Clinton presidential campaign strategists in 1992 seemed aware that there may be something to this theory. In campaign headquarters in Little Rock, Arkansas, James Carville hung up a sign that said "It's the Economy, Stupid"; hence the title of this chapter.

The theory as presented so far is hard to test because we do not generally observe voters' expectations of their future well-being. We must add to the theory an assumption about what influences these expectations. We will assume that the recent performance of the economy at the time of the election influences voters' expectations of their own future well-being. If the economy has been doing well, voters take this as a positive sign about their future well-being under the incumbent party. Conversely, if the economy has been doing poorly, voters take this as a negative sign. The theory and this assumption then imply that when the economy is doing well, voters tend to vote for the incumbent party, and when the economy is doing poorly, they tend to vote for the opposition party.

We now have something that can be tested. Does the incumbent party tend to do well when the economy is good and poorly when the economy is bad? Let's begin by taking as the measure of how the economy is doing the growth rate of output per person (real per capita Gross Domestic Product [GDP]) in the year of the election. Let's also use as the measure of how well the incumbent party does in an election the percentage of the two-party vote that it receives. For example, in 1996 the growth rate was 2.9 percent and the incumbent party's candidate (Bill Clinton) got 54.7 percent of the combined Democratic and Republican vote (and won). In 1992 the growth rate was 2.3 percent and the incumbent party's candidate (George Bush) got 46.6 percent of the combined two-party vote (and lost). (The reasons for using the two-party vote will be explained later.)

Figure 1-1 is a graph of the incumbent party vote share plotted against the growth rate for the 21 elections between 1916 and 1996 with the incumbent party vote share on the vertical axis and the growth rate on the horizontal axis. According to the above theory there should be a positive relationship between the two: when the growth rate is high, the vote share should be high, and vice versa.

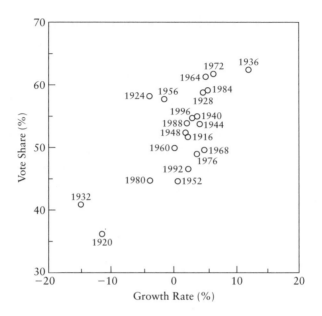

FIGURE **1-1**   Incumbent Party Vote Share Graphed Against the Growth Rate of
the Economy

Two cases that stand out in Figure 1-1 are the elections of 1932
and 1936. In 1932 the incumbent party's candidate (Herbert Hoover) got
40.8 percent of the two-party vote, a huge defeat in a year when the
growth rate of the economy was −14.9 percent (yes, that's a minus sign!).
In 1936 the incumbent party's candidate (Franklin Roosevelt) got
62.5 percent of the two-party vote, a huge victory in a year when the
growth rate of the economy was an exceptionally strong 11.9 percent.
(Although 1936 was in the decade of the Great Depression, the economy
actually grew quite rapidly in that year.)

Figure 1-1 shows that there does appear to be a positive relationship between the growth rate in the year of the election and the incumbent vote share: the scatter of points has an upward pattern. Voters may
thus take into account the state of the economy when deciding for whom
to vote, as the theory says.

The growth rate is not, however, the only measure of how well the
economy is doing. For example, inflation may also be of concern to
voters. When inflation has been high under the incumbent party, a voter

may fear that his or her income will not rise as fast as will prices in the future if the incumbent party's candidate is elected and thus that he or she will be worse off under the incumbent party. The voter may thus vote against the incumbent party. Many people consider inflation to be bad for their financial well-being, so high inflation may turn voters away from the incumbent party.

Deflation, which is falling prices, is also considered by many to be bad. People tend to like stable prices (that is, prices that on average don't change much from year to year). There have been some periods in U.S. history in which there was deflation. For example, prices on average declined during the four-year periods prior to the elections of 1924, 1928, and 1932. If voters dislike deflation as much as they dislike inflation, then inflation of −5 percent (which is deflation) is the same in the minds of the voters as inflation of +5 percent. Therefore, in dealing with the data on inflation, we will drop the minus sign when there is deflation. We are thus assuming that in terms of its impact on voters, a deflation of 5 percent is the same as an inflation of 5 percent.

To see how the incumbent party vote share and inflation are related, Figure 1-2 graphs the vote share against inflation. According to the theory just discussed, there should be a negative relationship between the two: when inflation is high, the vote share should be low, and vice versa. You can see from Figure 1-2 that there does seem to be at least a slight negative relationship between the incumbent party vote share and inflation: the scatter of points has a slight downward pattern. In 1980, for example, inflation was high (over 8 percent), and the vote share for the incumbent, President Carter, was low (less than 45 percent). In 1964, on the other hand, inflation was low (about 1 percent), and the vote share for the incumbent, President Johnson, was high (over 61 percent).

We are not, however, limited to a choice between one or the other, the growth rate or inflation. It may be that *both* the growth rate and inflation affect voting behavior. In other words, we need not assume that voters look at only one aspect of the economy when they are considering their future financial well-being. For example, if both the growth rate and inflation are high, a voter may be less inclined to vote for the incumbent party than if the growth rate is high and inflation is low. Similarly, if both the growth rate and inflation are low, a voter may be more inclined to vote for the incumbent party than if the growth rate is low and inflation is high.

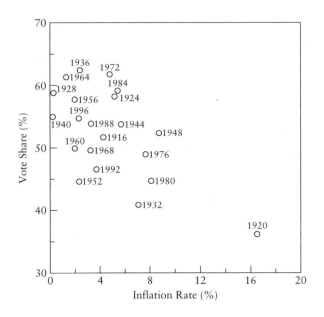

FIGURE **1-2**   Incumbent Party Vote Share Graphed Against the Inflation Rate

An example of a high growth rate and low inflation is 1964, where the growth rate was about 5 percent and inflation was about 1 percent. In this case the incumbent, President Johnson, won by a landslide over Barry Goldwater. An example of a low growth rate and high inflation is 1980, where the growth rate was about −4 percent and inflation was about 8 percent. In this case the incumbent, President Carter, lost by a large margin to Ronald Reagan.

To carry on, we are also not limited to only two measures of the health of the economy. In addition to observing how the economy has grown in the year of the election, voters may look at growth rates over the entire four years of the administration. In other words, past growth rates *along with the growth rate* in the election year may affect voting behavior. One measure of how good or bad past growth rates have been is the number of quarters during the four-year period of the administration in which the growth rate has exceeded some large number. These are quarters in which the output news was particularly good, and voters may be inclined to remember these kinds of events. There is some evidence from psychological experiments that people tend to remember peak stimuli more than they remember average stimuli, a finding that is consistent with voters remembering very strong growth quarters more than the others. Therefore, voters may be more inclined to vote for the incumbent party if there were many of these "good news" quarters during the administration than if there were few.

Noneconomic factors may also affect voting behavior. If the president is running for reelection, he (or maybe she in the future) may have a head start. He can perhaps use the power of the presidency to gain media attention, control events, and so forth. He is also presumably well known to voters, so there may be less uncertainty in voters' minds regarding the future if he is reelected rather than if someone new is elected. Voters who do not like uncertainty may thus be more inclined to vote for the incumbent party if the president is a candidate than otherwise.

It may also be that voters get tired, or bored, with a party if it has been in power for a long time, feeling that time has come for a change. Therefore, the longer a party has been in power, the less inclined voters may be to keep it in power. The vote share may thus depend on a measure of the duration of the incumbent party.

The theory of voting behavior that has just been presented can be summarized in Box 1-1.

BOX **1-1**

vote share depends on:	
	growth rate
	inflation
	good news quarters
	president running
	duration

The items in the box are called *variables*. A variable is something that changes, or varies. For example, the vote share is different for different elections; it varies across elections. Likewise, the growth rate is different for different elections; it also varies. Both the vote share and the growth rate are thus variables.

TABLE **1-1** Data Used for Explaining the Outcome of Presidential Elections, 1916–1996

Year	In Power	Election Outcome	Incumbent Vote Share (%)	Economic Growth Rate (%)	Inflation Rate (%)	Good News Quarters	Duration Value
1916	D	President Wilson beat Hughes	51.7	2.2	4.3	3	0.00
1920	D	Cox lost to Harding	36.1	−11.5	16.5	5	1.00
1924	R	President Coolidge beat Davis and La Follette	58.2	−3.9	5.2	10	0.00
1928	R	Hoover beat Smith	58.8	4.6	0.2	7	1.00
1932	R	President Hoover lost to F. Roosevelt	40.8	−14.9	7.1	4	1.25
1936	D	President F. Roosevelt beat Landon	62.5	11.9	2.4	9	0.00
1940	D	President F. Roosevelt beat Willkie	55.0	3.7	0.0	8	1.00
1944	D	President F. Roosevelt beat Dewey	53.8	4.1	5.7	14	1.25
1948	D	President Truman beat Dewey	52.4	1.8	8.7	5	1.50
1952	D	Stevenson lost to Eisenhower	44.6	0.6	2.3	6	1.75
1956	R	President Eisenhower beat Stevenson	57.8	−1.5	1.9	5	0.00
1960	R	Nixon lost to Kennedy	49.9	0.1	1.9	5	1.00
1964	D	President Johnson beat Goldwater	61.3	5.1	1.2	10	0.00
1968	D	Humphrey lost to Nixon	49.6	4.8	3.2	7	1.00
1972	R	President Nixon beat McGovern	61.8	6.3	4.8	4	0.00
1976	R	Ford lost to Carter	48.9	3.7	7.7	4	1.00
1980	D	President Carter lost to Reagan	44.7	−3.8	8.1	5	0.00
1984	R	President Reagan beat Mondale	59.2	5.4	5.4	7	0.00
1988	R	G. Bush beat Dukakis	53.9	2.1	3.3	6	1.00
1992	R	President G. Bush lost to Clinton	46.5	2.3	3.7	1	1.25
1996	D	President Clinton beat Dole	54.7	2.9	2.3	3	0.00

Note: See Chapter 3 for descriptions of the data.

The variable that is to be explained—in this case the vote share—is called the *dependent* variable. According to the theory, it "depends" on the other variables in the box. The other variables in the box—growth rate, inflation, good news quarters, president running, and duration—are called *independent* or *explanatory* variables. They help "explain" the dependent variable. The independent or explanatory variables are not themselves explained by the theory; they simply do the explaining.

The theory we have proposed may not, of course, capture well the way that voters actually behave. Maybe the economy plays no role. Maybe the vote share depends on a completely different set of factors—personality factors, foreign policy issues, social welfare issues, and so forth. We must collect data and test the theory.

The Data

To test the theory, we need data on past election outcomes and on what the economy was like for each election. We have already seen data on the vote share and the growth rate in Figure 1-1 and data on the vote share and inflation in Figure 1-2. Table 1-1 presents a more detailed picture of the data. The two-party vote share is presented for each election between 1916 and 1996, along with the growth rate, inflation rate, the number of good news quarters, and a measure of duration.

(Regarding the poem at the beginning of this chapter, William Jennings Bryan was the Democratic Party candidate in 1896, 1900, and 1908. He was defeated in the first two campaigns by William McKinley and in the 1908 campaign by William H. Taft. These elections are not in the sample in Table 1-1, but economic topics played a key role in Bryan's campaigns. In the election of 1896, for example, he made his famous cross of gold speech: "You shall not press down upon the brow of labor this crown of thorns, you shall not crucify mankind upon a cross of gold." The 1896 campaign in part pitted northeastern creditors against southern and western debtors. Bryan wanted the dollar to be backed by silver as well as gold, which would have put more money in circulation and led to lower interest rates, thus benefiting the South and West over the Northeast.)

The data in Table 1-1 are discussed in more detail in Chapter 3, so only a few points about the data will be made now. As mentioned above, in the periods before the elections of 1924, 1928, and 1932 inflation was negative (that is, there was deflation). Positive values are, however, listed in Table 1-1, reflecting the assumption that voters dislike deflation as much as they dislike inflation. If the president is running for reelection, this is indicated by the title "President" before the name. A candidate who was elected vice president and became president during the administration was counted as the president running for reelection. (Gerald Ford was not counted because he was not elected as vice president; he was appointed vice president after Spiro Agnew resigned.)

The duration variable in Table 1-1 has a value of 0.00 if the incumbent party has been in power only one term before the election. It has a value of 1.00 if the incumbent party has been in power two terms in a row, a value of 1.25 for three terms in a row, a value of 1.50 for four terms in a row, and a value of 1.75 for five terms in a row. We will use this variable in Chapter 3; it can be ignored for now.

Because we are taking the vote share to be the share of the *two-party* vote, we are ignoring possible third-party effects. We are in effect assuming that third-party votes are taken roughly equally from the two major parties. Again, we will come back to this in Chapter 3.

Table 1-1 gives a good picture of what is to be explained and the variables that the theory says may be important in the explanation. In the election of 1916 the incumbent party was Democratic, and President Wilson beat the Republican Hughes with 51.7 percent of the two-party vote. The growth rate was 2.2 percent, and inflation was 4.3 percent. In 1920 the incumbent party was Democratic and the Democrat Cox lost to the Republican Harding by a landslide. Cox got only 36.1 percent of the two-party vote. For this election the growth rate was −11.5 percent, and inflation was 16.5 percent—hardly a good economy! This outcome is, of course, consistent with the theory: the economy was very poor, and the incumbent party got trounced.

You may want to go through the rest of the elections and see what the story is for each. Only two more will be mentioned here. In 1980 President Carter lost to Reagan with a vote share of 44.7 percent. The economy was not good for Carter: The growth rate was −3.8 percent and inflation was 8.1 percent. This outcome is again consistent with the theory. On the other hand, the theory has trouble with the 1992 election, where President George Bush lost to Clinton with a vote share of

46.5 percent. Unlike 1980, the economy was not that bad in 1992: the growth rate was 2.3 percent and inflation was 3.7 percent. There is thus a puzzle as to why President Bush lost, or at least why he lost by as much as he did. We will return to this question in Chapter 3.

On to the Tools

We have presented a theory of voting behavior in this chapter, and we have presented data that can be used to test the theory. This is, however, as far as we can go without the tools, so it is on to Chapter 2. Once the tools have been explained in Chapter 2, they will be used in Chapter 3 to test the theory of voting behavior and in Chapter 4 to predict future elections.

Plato, despair!
We prove by norms
How numbers bear
Empiric forms,

How random wrong
Will average right
If time be long
And error slight,

But in our hearts
Hyperbole
Curves and departs
To infinity.

Error is boundless.
Nor hope nor doubt,
Though both be groundless,
Will average out.

J. V. Cunningham, Meditation on Statistical Method

MONDAY
Lesson 1: Begin with a Theory

We begin with a theory of what we are trying to explain. In the previous chapter a theory of voting behavior was presented—a theory of what motivates people to vote the way they do. Although it does not matter where a theory comes from, the theory should have a ring of plausibility. A theory that seems completely at odds with how something works is not of much interest to test and is not likely to get us very far.

It is easiest to explain the following tools using a particular theory as an example, and we will use the theory of voting behavior. To begin, we will simplify matters and assume that the vote share depends only on the economy's growth rate in the year of the election. The theory we begin with is that the growth rate has a positive effect on the incumbent party vote share.

TUESDAY
Lesson 2: Collect Data

Empirical evidence or information is needed to test a theory. This requires collecting observations on the variable to be explained (the dependent variable) and the variables that, according to the theory, do the explaining (the independent or explanatory variables). Observations on variables are called *data*. Table 1-1 provides a good example of data collection. Observations are available for the period 1916–1996 on the vote share, the growth rate, and a number of other variables. This table contains the data that we will use to test the theory of voting behavior.

Data collection is perhaps the most important step in testing a theory. A good test requires that the variables for which observations are collected match closely the variables that the theory is talking about. It is not always easy to find good matches, and much of social science research consists of the nitty gritty job of finding appropriate data. Tuesday is thus a critical day. Always keep in mind when deciding how much to trust the results of a test that a test is no better than the data behind it.

WEDNESDAY
Lesson 3: Fit the Data

This is the hardest lesson except for Lesson 4. If you have not had this kind of material before—essentially fitting points to a line—you may need to go through it more than once. Keep in mind that the main aim of this lesson is to fit as closely as possible the theory from Lesson 1 to the data from Lesson 2.

We begin with Table 1-1, where we have 21 observations on the vote share and on the growth rate. In Figure 2-1 the vote share is graphed against the growth rate. This is the same graph as Figure 1-1, although now we are going to do more with it. The vote share is on the vertical axis, and the growth rate is on the horizontal axis.

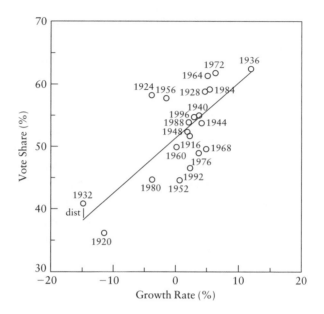

FIGURE **2-1** **Incumbent Party Vote Share Graphed Against the Growth Rate of the Economy**

Note that the points in Figure 2-1 have an upward pattern (rising from left to right). In other words, the vote share tends to be larger the larger the growth rate. This is, of course, exactly what our theory says should be the case. In some cases, however, one vote share is larger than another, even though it has a smaller growth rate associated with it. For example, the vote share for 1956 is larger than the vote share for 1996, even though the growth rate for 1956 is smaller than that for 1996. It is clear that the points in the figure do not all lie on a straight line, and in this sense the relationship between the vote share and the growth rate is not exact.

Even though all the points in Figure 2-1 do not lie on a straight line, we can ask which straight line the points are closest to. Put another way, we can ask which line best "fits" the points. To see what is involved in finding the best fitting line, consider drawing some line through the points, such as the line drawn in the figure. You should think for now of this line as being any arbitrary line, not necessarily the best fitting line. Some points on the particular line in the figure, such as the one for 1940, are almost exactly on the line. Others, such as the one for 1920, are farther away from the line. The vertical distance between a point and the line, such as that labelled *dist* for 1932, is a measure of how far the point is from the line. This distance is sometimes called an *error*. If all points were exactly on the line, all errors would be zero, and the relationship between the vote share and the growth rate would be exact. Otherwise, the larger the distances are on average, the less precise is the relationship.

The errors corresponding to the points that are below the line are negative, and the errors corresponding to the points that are above the line are positive. In other words, relative to the line some points are too low, and some points are too high. Now, if we change the sign of the negative errors to positive and add up all the errors, the answer (the sum) is a measure of how closely the line fits the points. We are just adding up all the distances of the points from the line. One line can be said to fit better than another line if it has a smaller sum. In practice, a more popular way of measuring how well a line fits the points is first to take each error and square it (that is, multiply each error by itself) and then to add up all the squared errors. Either way, the general idea is the same. In terms of deciding which line fits best, a line in which the points are far from the line (that is, when the distances from the points to the line are large) is not as good as a line in which the points are close to the line.

We will follow the convention of squaring the errors before summing them. Now, imagine drawing thousands of straight lines in Figure 2-1, each with a different position in the figure, and for each line taking the 21 errors, squaring them, and then adding up the squared errors. We can thus associate one number (the sum of the errors squared) with each line, and this number is a measure of how well that particular line fits the points. If the number for a given line is large relative to numbers for other lines, this means that the given line is not positioned well in the figure. For this line the distances from the points to the line are on average large, so the line does not fit the points well. The best fitting line out of the thousands of lines is simply the line with the smallest number (that is, the smallest sum of squared errors). Although it would take hours to draw thousands of lines by hand and compute the number for each line, computers can find the best fitting line very quickly. It takes almost no time for a computer to find the line with the smallest sum of squared errors.

Assume that we have found the best fitting line with the help of a computer. (This is in fact the line drawn in Figure 2-1.) Associated with this line is, of course, its sum of squared errors. Although the sum of squared errors is a measure of how well the line fits the points, it does not give one a sense of what a typical error is. A better sense of the size of a typical error can be obtained by dividing the sum of squared errors by the number of observations, which gives the average squared error, and then taking the square root of the average squared error, which gives the average error. It turns out, for example, that the sum of squared errors for the line in Figure 2-1 is 461.6. If we divide this number by 21, the number of points in the figure, we get 22.0, which is the average squared error. If we then take the square root of this number, we get 4.7, which is the average error.

Although we might use the average error of 4.7 as the measure of a typical error, in practice a slightly different measure is used. In the present example instead of dividing the sum of squared errors of 461.6 by 21, we divide it by 19. In other words, we subtract 2 from the number of points before dividing. We use 2 because the line is determined by 2 points. If there were only 2 points in Figure 2-1, the line would fit perfectly—2 zero errors. So we start off in this sense with 2 zero errors, leaving 19 to play with. If we divide 461.6 by 19, we get 24.3. The square root of this number is 4.9, slightly larger than our earlier value of 4.7. We then take 4.9 as the measure of a typical error. This error measure is sometimes called a *standard error*, and we will use this terminology. A *standard error* is just a measure of the average size of a typical error for a line like that in Figure 2-1.

Is the standard error of 4.9 for the line in Figure 2-1 large or small? We can see from Table 1-1 in the previous chapter that the vote share ranges from a low of 36.1 percent in 1920 to a high of 62.5 percent in 1936. The difference between the high and the low is thus 26.4, so 4.9 is fairly small compared to this range. On the other hand, many elections have been decided with a margin of less than 4.9 percentage points, so on this score 4.9 is fairly large. We will see in the next chapter that when the other explanatory variables are taken into account, the standard error is much smaller than 4.9. For now, however, we will stay with using only the growth rate and thus the standard error of 4.9.

We have so far found the best fitting line and calculated the standard error. Another way to get a sense of how well the line fits the points is simply to examine individual points. In particular, it is of interest to see which points are far from the line (that is, which points have large errors associated with them). For example, the error for the election of 1924 is quite large, as we can see in Figure 2-1. For this election the vote share is high, and the growth rate is low (in fact negative), resulting in a point far above the line. The election of 1956 is a similar case, where the vote share is high, and the growth rate is low. A point that is relatively far below the line is 1952, where the vote share is low and the growth rate modest. On the other hand, a number of points—such as 1988, 1996, 1940, and 1936—are virtually on the line.

Another useful number we can get from Figure 2-1 is the *slope* of the line. The *slope* of a line is the measure of how steep it is. The slope of the line in Figure 2-1 is positive: it rises upward and to the right. A negative slope is one in which the line moves downward and to the right. The slope of the line in Figure 2-1 is 0.9. This means that if you move along the horizontal axis by one unit, the vote share on the line will increase by 0.9 units. For example, an increase in the growth rate of 1.0 percentage points will increase the vote share by 0.9 percentage points on the line.

You can probably see already why the size of the slope is important. If the slope is large (that is, the line is steep), the growth rate has a large effect on the vote share according to the line. If, on the other hand, the slope is zero (that is, the line is horizontal), the growth rate has no effect on the vote share according to the line. Clearly, if the slope in Figure 2-1 were zero or close to zero, there would be no support for the theory that the growth rate affects the vote share.

The slope of the best fitting line is sometimes called the *estimated slope,* and we will use this terminology. The slope is estimated in the sense that it is computed by finding the best fitting line given whatever observations are at our disposal.

This is it for Lesson 3. The basic idea is to see how well a theory fits the data. In the simple case considered so far of a dependent variable and one explanatory variable, the theory is used to choose the two variables (in our example the vote share and the growth rate). The data are then used to find the best fitting line. The main point of this lesson is to show how best fitting lines are found.

Lesson 4: Test

Just because we have found the best fitting line does not mean we have discovered anything interesting or useful. One of the main things social scientists worry about when analyzing relationships such as the one between the vote share and the growth rate is that a relationship may have been uncovered by coincidence and that it is in fact not truly valid. In the present example we worry that the vote share is not really affected by the growth rate even though for our 21 observations it looks like it is.

One way to state our anxiety is by saying that we are worried that the true slope of the line in a figure like Figure 2-1 is zero. If the true slope is zero, there is no relationship between the growth rate and the vote share. Although the slope of the line in Figure 2-1 is positive, as the theory of voting behavior says it should be, it may be that the positive slope is just a fluke. It may be just by chance that the 21 available observations (points) show a positive effect. If we had 21 other observations (say by waiting for 21 more elections to take place), they might show a much smaller positive slope or even a negative slope. We need to test whether the positive slope is or is not a fluke.

The main point of this lesson is to explain how we can test whether the true slope is zero. As noted at the end of Lesson 3, the slope in Figure 2-1 is 0.9, and we want to see how likely it is that the true slope is zero, even though we have estimated it to be 0.9. We will see that we can compute for an estimated slope its *t-statistic*. We will then see that if the value of the *t*-statistic is greater than about 2.0, it is very unlikely that the true slope is zero. A *t*-statistic greater than 2.0 is thus good for the theory. It says that the slope we have estimated by finding the best fitting line is unlikely to be truly zero.

The rest of this lesson is hard, and if you are willing to take the result about the *t*-statistic on faith, you may skip to Lesson 5. Or you may skip this material for now and come back later, once you have seen, in Chapters 3 and beyond, the use of *t*-statistics in action.

Thursday Morning

We begin with the errors in Figure 2-1. Remember that an error for a point is the distance from the point to the line. Also remember that an error is negative if the point is below the line and positive if the point is above the line. Now, say that instead of 21 errors, we had hundreds of them (from hundreds of elections), and we recorded how many of them were between 0.0 and 0.1, how many were between 0.1 and 0.2, how many were between −0.1 and 0.0, and so on. In other words, say that we have intervals of size 0.1 and we record how many errors are in each interval: we record how many very small errors there are, how many fairly small errors, how many medium errors, and so on.

In most cases we will find that there are more very small errors than small ones, more small errors than medium ones, more medium errors than large ones, and so on. In fact, in many cases if we graph the number of errors in each interval against the position of the interval on the horizontal axis, we will get points that lie on a curve which is approximately like that in Figure 2-2. The curve in Figure 2-2 is a bell-shaped curve,

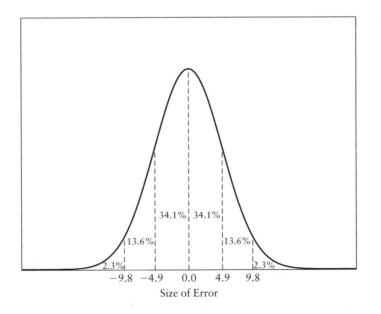

FIGURE **2-2** Bell-Shaped Curve for Errors in Figure 2-1

which is a curve you may have seen in other contexts. If, for example, you divided scores on intelligence tests (IQ scores) into small intervals and graphed the number of scores in each interval against the position of the interval on the horizontal axis, you would get points that lie approximately on a bell-shaped curve.

We will assume that the curve in Figure 2-2 is an exact bell-shaped curve. We will also assume that the peak of the bell-shaped curve corresponds to an error of zero and that the standard error, as computed in Lesson 3, is 4.9. A bell-shaped curve has some useful characteristics concerning the size of the area under the curve that we need to know about. The total area under the curve is the space under the curve and above the horizontal axis. Consider starting from zero and moving a distance of 4.9 to the right and 4.9 to the left, where 4.9 is the standard error. Doing this sweeps out 34.1 percent of the area to the right of zero and 34.1 percent of the area to the left of zero, for a total of 68.2 percent of the area under the curve. This area is shown in Figure 2-2. In other words, 68.2 percent of the errors are between −4.9 and 4.9, where again 4.9 is the standard error.

If we sweep out the area between 4.9 and 9.8, we get another 13.6 percent, and if we sweep out the area between −4.9 and −9.8 we get another 13.6 percent. The total area between −9.8 and 9.8 is thus 95.4 percent. Looked at another way, the area to the right of 9.8 is 2.3 percent, and the area to the left of −9.8 is 2.3 percent. In other words, for a bell-shaped curve with a standard error of 4.9, only 2.3 percent of the errors are larger than 9.8 and only 2.3 percent are smaller than −9.8.

So, you might ask, why are you telling me this? In particular, what does this have to do with the question of whether the positive slope in Figure 2-1 is a fluke? Well, we are making progress, but patience is still needed. The next step is to consider the following thought experiment: Imagine another universe in which there were 21 presidential elections with the same 21 growth rates as in Figure 2-1. If this universe were identical to ours, the vote shares would also be the same, and Figure 2-1 would pertain exactly to both universes. But for our thought experiment we would like the other universe to have different errors.

Consider, for example, the 1992 election, where President George Bush lost to candidate Bill Clinton. As in any election, there were many things that affected voting behavior aside from the growth rate, and for this election these other things were on net negative for Bush. This can be seen by noting that the point for 1992 in Figure 2-1 is below the line. Remember that the distance from a point to the line is the error for that point. Because the point for 1992 is below the line, the error is negative. Although not directly recorded in Figure 2-1, the error for 1992 is −7.0 percent, which is fairly large. In 1992 President Bush got 46.5 percent of the two-party vote, which is the 1992 point in Figure 2-1. The position on the line corresponding to the 1992 growth rate is 53.5 percent. The −7.0 error is the difference between 46.5 and 53.5. In the present context we can look upon an error in any given election as reflecting all the other things that affect voting behavior aside from the growth rate. The more these other things matter, the larger on average will the error be. We have, fortunately, a measure of how large the errors are on average, which is the standard error of 4.9.

Now comes the key step. We want to draw a different error for the 1992 election from the one that actually occurred (which was −7.0). We are going to draw this error from a bell-shaped curve with a standard error of 4.9. This error will generally be different from the actual error of −7.0, so the vote share in this universe will be different from the vote share of 46.5 percent in the actual universe. We are imagining an election in 1992 in the other universe with the same growth rate but with a different set of the other things that affect voting behavior. Maybe in the other universe more people were repulsed by Clinton's flying back to Arkansas during the New Hampshire primary to make sure that Ricky Ray Rector—the death row inmate whose brain had been partially destroyed by a gunshot wound and who appeared not to understand what was happening—was executed, leading fewer people to vote for him in the general election. Or maybe Bush successfully toppled Saddam Hussein in the Gulf War, leading more people to vote for him. We are thus imagining a different set of other things, which implies a different error, and we are drawing this error at random from a bell-shaped curve with a standard error of 4.9. By using a standard error of 4.9, we are assuming that the same bell-shaped curve pertains to the other universe as pertains to ours. In other words, the average size of the effect of the "other things" is assumed to be the same.

We draw an error not only for 1992 but for the other 20 elections as well, each time using the bell-shaped curve with a standard error of 4.9. Drawing the 21 errors gives us 21 points that are different from those in Figure 2-1. With this new figure we can find the line that best fits the points. Because the points are different, the best fitting line will generally be in a different position from the line in Figure 2-1. So generally it will also have a different slope. We thus have two estimated slopes—the original slope of 0.9 and the new slope.

We now go to a third universe and draw a new set of 21 errors. We get a new figure, and we find the best fitting line for the new figure. The slope of this line is our third estimated slope. We keep doing this until we have run through many universes, say 1,000. We have thus computed 1,000 different estimated slopes.

The next step is to examine the 1,000 slopes. As we did above for the errors, we divide these slopes into small intervals and then graph the number of slopes in each interval against the position of the interval on the horizontal axis. When we do this, we get points that lie approximately on a bell-shaped curve. This curve is drawn in Figure 2-3. We will assume that this curve is exactly bell-shaped. In practice it is not quite bell-shaped, but for most applications the bell-shaped curve is a very close approximation.

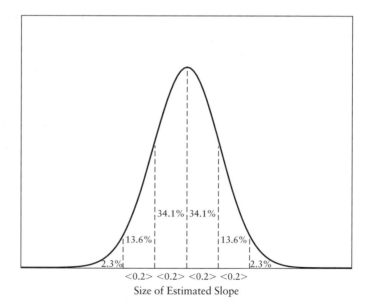

FIGURE **2-3 Bell-Shaped Curve for Estimated Slopes**

It is important to keep in mind that we have moved from errors to slopes. The bell-shaped curve in Figure 2-2 is for the errors from Figure 2-1 (that is, the distances from the points to the line), whereas the bell-shaped curve in Figure 2-3 is for the slopes we have estimated from our different universes.

We use the bell-shaped curve in Figure 2-3 in the following way. We start from the estimated slope that is exactly under the peak of the curve, and we sweep out 34.1 percent of the area to the right. We know from the characteristic of a bell-shaped curve that the distance we travel along the horizontal axis to sweep out 34.1 percent of the area is one standard error. In the present example this distance turns out to be 0.2. This means that the standard error of the estimated slope is 0.2. As shown in the figure, if we move another 0.2 to the right, we sweep out 13.6 percent of the area. If we move left from the center by 0.2, we sweep out 34.1 percent of the area, and if we move left another 0.2, we sweep out another 13.6 percent of the area.

This standard error of 0.2 for the estimated slope in Figure 2-3 is, of course, different from the standard error of 4.9 in Figure 2-2, which is for the line in Figure 2-1. Each bell-shaped curve has its own standard error. We need to always be clear in what follows as to which standard error we are talking about. When there is a possible confusion, we will use the phrases *standard error of the line* and *standard error of the estimated slope*.

Let us recap what we have done so far. The slope of the line in Figure 2-1, which is 0.9, depends on the particular set of 21 points in the figure. If there were a different set of 21 points, the slope would generally be different. We can get a measure of how sensitive the estimated slope is to different sets of points by computing many slope values (from many hypothetical universes). Once we have computed many slope values, we can use the bell-shaped curve to find the standard error of the estimated slope. This standard error is a measure of the sensitivity of the estimated slope to different sets of points. The bell-shaped curve in Figure 2-3 is needed only to compute the standard error of the estimated slope, namely by sweeping out 34.1 percent of the area from the center and computing the distance traveled along the horizontal axis. In practice the standard error of the estimated slope is computed in a way that does not require drawing errors from hypothetical universes, but the answer is the same in either case. In other words, the 0.2 standard error is trivial to compute.

We still have one more key step to take, but you may want to take a break for lunch before finishing. You should have a good idea of what the standard error of the estimated slope is before reading further.

Thursday Afternoon

The main thing we are worried about from the point of view of the theory of voting behavior is whether the true slope in Figure 2-1 is zero. If the slope is truly zero, this means that the growth rate has no effect on the vote share: changes in the growth rate have no effect on the vote share if the line is completely flat. If the slope is zero, then the theory is not supported by the data.

Fortunately, we can now test whether the slope is zero. This is done in Figure 2-4. The figure is based on the assumption that the true slope is zero. We know from Figure 2-1 that the slope we have computed

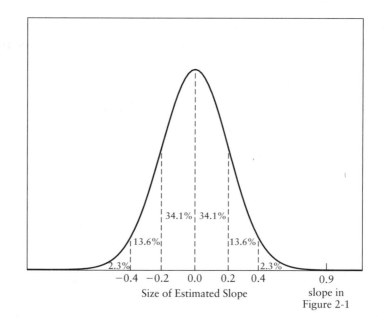

FIGURE **2-4** Bell-Shaped Curve for Estimated Slopes if True Slope Were Zero

is 0.9. In order to test whether 0.9 is a fluke, we need to know the chance that we would get a value of 0.9 if the true slope were zero. This is where we need our standard error of the estimated slope of 0.2. Figure 2-4 shows that it is very unlikely with a standard error of 0.2 that we would get an estimated slope of 0.9 if the true slope were zero. The probability that we would get a slope of 0.9 if the true slope were zero is the area under the curve to the right of 0.9 in the figure, which is very close to zero. (The area is so small that it can't even be seen in the figure!) The data thus support the theory that the growth rate affects the vote share. To repeat, if the growth rate did not affect the vote share, it is unlikely we would get a slope of 0.9 in Figure 2-1. It is thus likely that the theory is true.

Now comes the punch line. If we divide the slope (0.9) by the standard error of the estimated slope (0.2), we get what is called a *t-statistic* (4.5 in this example). The *t*-statistic is a highly useful concept. Assume for the sake of argument that we had an estimated slope of 0.4 instead of 0.9, with the same standard error of 0.2. This would mean that the *t*-statistic is 2.0. We can see from Figure 2-4 that for an estimated slope of 0.4, the area under the curve that lies to the right of it is 2.3 percent. Therefore, the probability that we would get a slope of 0.4 if the true slope were zero (and the standard error of the estimated slope were 0.2) is just 2.3 percent. For a *t*-statistic of 2.0 it is thus unlikely that the true slope is zero and thus likely that the theory is true. In practice, a *t*-statistic of 2.0, or around 2.0, is used as a cutoff in deciding whether a theory is supported or not. A theory is not supported if the *t*-statistic is less than 2.0 or thereabouts, and a theory is supported if the *t*-statistic is greater than 2.0 or thereabouts. This convention is, of course, somewhat arbitrary, and other cutoffs could be used. A *t*-statistic of less than 2.0 would mean more theories would be supported, and a *t*-statistic of greater than 2.0, fewer. We will use a cutoff of 2.0 in this book.

If a slope is negative, the *t*-statistic is negative. In this case the cutoff is a *t*-statistic of −2.0. A *t*-statistic of less than −2.0 (such as −3.0) means that it is unlikely that the true slope is zero, so a theory that said that the slope was negative would be supported.

Using a cutoff of 2.0 (or −2.0), an estimated slope is said to be *significant* if it has a *t*-statistic greater than 2.0 (or less than −2.0). *Significant* means it is unlikely that the true slope is zero. *Significant* is also used sometimes to refer to a variable that has a significant estimated slope. In our present example, the growth rate is significant because the *t*-statistic of the estimated slope is 4.5, which is greater than the cutoff of 2.0. The results are summarized in Box 2-1.

BOX **2-1**

vote share depends on:		*t*-statistic
0.9	growth rate	4.5
51.4	intercept	46.7
standard error: 4.9		
number of observations: 21		

The estimated slope of the line is 0.9, and it has a *t*-statistic of 4.5. Since the *t*-statistic is greater than 2.0, we can say that the growth rate is significant. The standard error of the line, a measure of a typical error, is 4.9, and there are 21 points, or observations.

The term in the box that we have not yet discussed is the *intercept*. The line in Figure 2-1 has both a slope and an intercept. The *intercept* is the point on the line where the growth rate is zero. When we find the best fitting line, we find both its slope and its intercept. The intercept has a standard error associated with it just like the slope does, and its standard error can be computed in the same way as was done for the slope's standard error. Once the intercept's standard error is computed, its *t*-statistic can be computed. As can be seen in the box, the *t*-statistic of the intercept is 46.7, which is huge. Not surprisingly, the data strongly reject the case that the true intercept is zero. The intercept is 51.4, which means that if the growth rate were zero, the vote share would be 51.4 percent according to the line. The line thus says that the incumbent party wins by a small margin if the growth rate is zero.

As a final point, it is important to see how the size of a *t*-statistic is related to the size of the standard error of the line, both of which are presented in the box. Consider, for example, a case in which the points in Figure 2-1 lie on average much closer to the line than is actually the case in the figure. In particular, say that the size of a typical error (that is, the standard error of the line), is 1.9 rather than 4.9. This means that the bell-shaped curve in Figure 2-2 is much less spread out. Now when we are computing the standard error of the estimated slope by drawing many sets of 21 errors (from many universes), the errors are on average smaller, so the estimated slopes are on average closer to the slope of 0.9. In other words, the best fitting lines move around less in the different universes because the new points are closer to the original points. This means that the standard error of the estimated slope will be smaller (Figure 2-3 will be less spread out). Therefore, the *t*-statistic of the slope will be larger. This, of course, makes sense. If the errors in Figure 2-1 are on average small, we have more confidence that the slope is not a fluke than if the errors are on average large.

We are finally done with Lesson 4. We have shown how to test whether the true slope of a line is zero given the slope that was computed by finding the best fitting line. The test is to compute the *t*-statistic of the estimated slope and see if it is greater than 2.0 or less than -2.0. If it is, then it is unlikely that the true slope is zero, which is support for the theory. One should not, however, get carried away with this result. The test is not necessarily the final answer, which is the subject matter of Lesson 5.

FRIDAY
Lesson 5: Think About Pitfalls

Since the *t*-statistic for the growth rate in our example is much greater than 2.0, are we almost positive that the growth rate affects the vote share? Figure 2-4 would suggest yes, since there is a very small probability that we would get a slope of 0.9 if the true slope were zero. Alas, life is not quite this simple. Mistakes are possible that would not be caught by the test using the *t*-statistic. The theory may be wrong even with a *t*-statistic of 4.5. The following are possible pitfalls that you need to be aware of even with large *t*-statistics.

Say the truth is that what affects the vote share is not the growth rate but the size of the armed forces. The size of the armed forces is large during wars, and if people rally around the flag during wars, they may be more inclined to vote for the incumbent party during wars than they would otherwise. Wars also tend to stimulate the economy, so the growth rate is on average higher during wars than at other times. The growth rate and the size of the armed forces thus tend to move together: when one is high, the other tends to be high, and when one is low, the other tends to be low. If this is true, then high growth rates will be associated with large vote shares, and low growth rates will be associated with small vote shares. We may thus get a pattern of points like that in Figure 2-1, namely an upward pattern, but what is really affecting the vote share is not the growth rate but the size of the armed forces. We would be fooling ourselves in thinking that the growth rate is the cause. We thus have to be careful that the variable we think is affecting the vote share is not in fact acting as a proxy for something else.

It may also be that *both* the growth rate and the size of the armed forces affect the vote share. In other words, there may be both a rally-around-the-flag effect and a separate growth-rate effect. We will discuss how to treat two explanatory variables instead of just one later in this chapter. What we can say now is that if both variables matter but only the growth rate is included, the growth rate will get too much credit regarding its effect on the vote share. The estimated slope will be too large because, by omitting the size of the armed forces, the growth rate is picking up part of the effect of the size of the armed forces on the vote share. This problem is called *omitted variable bias*. The estimated slope for an explanatory variable is wrong (biased) because some other explanatory variable has been omitted that truly affects the dependent variable, one that is also related to the included explanatory variable.

The use of polling results provides an example of another possible pitfall. Say that for each election one had polling data one week before the election. If in a figure like Figure 2-1 one graphed the vote share against the polling results, there is likely to be an upward pattern and fairly small errors on average around the best fitting line. Polls are usually fairly accurate one week before the election. The slope of the best fitting line is likely to be positive and have a large *t*-statistic. It is not the case, however, that the polling results are *causing* the voters to vote the way they do. The polls are just asking voters one week ahead how they are going to vote. Therefore, good fits and large *t*-statistics do not guarantee that one has explained anything.

Another possible pitfall is that voting behavior may have changed sometime during the period of the data. Possibly the true slope was large during the 1916–44 period and small (perhaps zero) after that. Figure 2-1 would be incorrectly showing that the true slope is the same for both periods. Although this mistake will make the average error larger than it would be if there were no shift of behavior, it may still be that the *t*-statistic for the estimated slope turns out to be greater than 2.0. Possible shifting behavior is a nightmare for social scientists trying to explain behavior over time, because stability is needed to learn very much.

It may also be that the true relationship is not a straight line in Figure 2-1, but a curved line. Maybe the line begins to curve up at a growth rate of about 5 percent. Incorrectly using a straight line may still result in a positive estimated slope and a *t*-statistic greater than 2.0.

Another interesting way in which we might be fooled goes under the name of *data mining*. Say that we have observations on 100 possible variables that we think may affect the vote share. We try each variable, one by one, and see what its estimated slope and *t*-statistic are. Let's say we then pick the variable with the largest *t*-statistic and conclude that this variable affects the vote share. The potential problem with this procedure should be obvious. By trying so many variables, it is likely that just by chance we have found one that results in a good fit and an estimated slope with a *t*-statistic greater than 2.0. In other words, even if none of the 100 variables truly affect the vote share, we may find some that by chance fit well.

There are two ways to mitigate the data mining problem. One is to use theory to narrow down the number of variables to try. Stupid variables, such as a candidate's eye color, can be eliminated. We can use theory to narrow the list of possible variables to those that have some plausibility. The other way concerns prediction, which is the topic of Lesson 7.

To conclude, we must take any *t*-statistic with a grain of salt. High *t*-statistics are not a guarantee of success, and any result must be examined carefully for possible pitfalls.

SATURDAY
Lesson 6: Examine the Results

If the tests of a theory reveal that the data do not support it, then this lesson and the next one are of no interest. It is of no interest to examine results like the size of the slope or to use the slope to make predictions if the theory is not supported. Similarly, if the possible pitfalls seem really serious, we may not want to continue even if the theory were supported using the tests in Lesson 4. We need to have some confidence in the theory before we can use it.

If the results are supportive of a theory and the possible pitfalls do not seem serious, the next step is to examine the implications of the results. In Figure 2-1, for example, it is of interest to see what the line says about the size of the effect of the growth rate on the vote share. If, say, the growth rate increases from 2.0 percent to 3.0 percent, how much does the line say the vote share should increase? We have already answered this question in our discussion of the slope at the end of Lesson 3. The size of the effect is measured by the slope of the line. A steep slope implies a much larger effect than does a mild slope. The slope of the line in Figure 2-1 is 0.9. The line thus tells us that if the growth rate increases by 1.0, the vote share should increase by 0.9. If the slope were instead steeper, say 1.5, then an increase in the growth rate of 1.0 would mean that the vote share should increase by 1.5.

A slope of 0.9 is fairly large in the context of this example. For example, we can see in Table 1-1 that the growth rate was −3.8 percent in 1980 and 5.4 percent in 1984, which is a difference of 9.2. A change in the growth rate of 9.2 implies, according to the line, that the vote share should change by 0.9 times 9.2, or 8.3, which is a large change in the vote share. It is interesting to note that the actual vote share was 44.7 percent in 1980 (President Carter lost to Reagan) and 59.2 percent in 1984 (President Reagan beat Mondale), a difference of 14.5. The actual change in the vote share was thus larger than 8.3, but the line got quite a bit of the increase.

In our simple example here all we really have to examine is the size of the slope, which we have done. In most applications there is more to be done (that is, more implications of the results to consider). We will see examples in the following chapters.

SUNDAY
Lesson 7: Predict

Once we have done all the above work, prediction is easy and fun. We must not get too excited, however. The possible pitfalls we discussed in Lesson 5 are always lurking in the shadows, and we must not get overconfident.

Say that we want to use the line in Figure 2-1 to predict the 2000 election, which was not one of the 21 observations (the last election used was 1996). To make a prediction we must first choose a value for the growth rate. Say we are making a prediction in January 2000, and we think the growth rate in 2000 will be 3.0 percent. We know, from Box 2-1, that the intercept is 51.4. This means that the value of the vote share on the line at a growth rate of 0.0 is 51.4. How much will the vote share increase if the growth rate is 3.0 rather than 0.0? Since the slope is 0.9, the vote share increases by 0.9 times 3.0, or 2.7. The vote share on the line at a growth rate of 3.0 is thus 51.4 plus 2.7, or 54.1. The incumbent party (Democratic) is thus predicted to win with 54.1 percent of the vote for a growth rate of 3.0 percent.

Say instead you thought in January 2000 that there was going to be a recession in 2000, possibly because of a stock market crash, and that the growth rate was going to be −3.0. In this case the predicted vote share is 51.4 minus 2.7, or 48.7, which would mean a Republican victory.

It is thus easy to make a prediction. Pick a growth rate, and find out where on the line in Figure 2-1 you are for this growth rate. Note that any prediction assumes that the error for 2000 will be zero (that is, the vote share will be exactly on the line). This is where we need to be cautious. A typical error is 4.9 (the standard error of the line), so the actual outcome could differ from the predicted value by quite a bit. The standard error of 4.9 incorporates all the factors that affect voting behavior other than the growth rate, and these other factors have on average an effect of 4.9 on the vote share. You can see from Figure 2-2 that 68.2 percent of the time the error will be between −4.9 and 4.9. So with a predicted vote share of 54.1 percent, we can say that 68.2 percent of the time the actual vote share will be between 49.2 and 59.0 percent. This is, of course, a fairly wide range. (We will see in the next chapter that the range narrows considerably when we depart from assuming that the vote share depends *only* on the growth rate.)

In addition to taking into account the size of the standard error of the line when thinking about a prediction, we must also be cautious about the possible pitfalls from Lesson 5. If any of the pitfalls are relevant, we will at a minimum be using a standard error that is too small.

Prediction can help us see if the data mining problem is serious, at least if we are willing to wait for another observation. Say that by trying many variables we have found a variable that fits the 21 elections very well. If the truth is that this variable has no effect on the vote share, then the line that we have chosen is not likely to predict the next election well.

We have searched using the 21 elections to find a line that looks good, but it is in fact spurious. Because the line is spurious, there is no reason to think it will do well for the next election, since the next election's outcome has not been used in the search. Observing how well a line predicts outside the period of the fit is thus a way of checking for possible data mining problems.

We have one more very important point to make about prediction. Remember that all we need to make a prediction of the vote share is a value for the growth rate. We used values of 3.0 and −3.0 above, but we could easily use other values. Once the actual growth rate for 2000 is known, we can also use it. (At the time of this writing the actual growth rate is known, but this is material for Chapter 4.) In terms of testing the theory, the actual growth rate should obviously be used. We want to compare the actual vote share for 2000 with the predicted vote share using the actual growth rate for 2000. Using any other growth rate would not be a test of the theory because the test would be based on an incorrect growth rate.

There is thus an important difference between (1) predicting ahead of time (such as in January 2000), where the actual value of the growth rate is not known, and (2) predicting after the fact, where the actual value is known. When we predict ahead, we must already have some predicted value of the growth rate to use. In other words, we must predict (somehow) the growth rate ahead of the vote share. It is somewhat unfortunate, but *predict* is used for both of these types of predictions. When it is important to distinguish between the two, we will refer to the first prediction as a *real-time* prediction and to the second prediction as an *after-the-fact* prediction. *Real-time predictions* are predictions in actual forecasting situations where the actual outcomes are not known. *After-the-fact predictions* are predictions based on the actual values of the explanatory variables (the growth rate in the present example).

One last point. An after-the-fact prediction can be made for any observation in the sample period. In other words, an after-the-fact prediction can be made for any of the 21 elections in Table 1-1 once the slope and intercept are estimated. This can be done because we know the actual value of the growth rate for each election. We just take the intercept, which is 51.4 from Box 2-1, and add to it 0.9 times the actual growth rate, where 0.9 is the estimated slope in Box 2-1. We in fact did this above when we were discussing the 1992 election. The after-the-fact predicted value for President Bush in 1992 is 51.4 plus 0.9 times 2.3, which is 53.5, where 2.3 is the actual value of the growth rate. The actual value of the vote share is 46.5 percent, so the error is 7.0 percent. We can thus say that an error for any observation is simply the difference between the after-the-fact predicted value and the actual value.

Adding More Variables

The lessons in this chapter have been presented under the assumption that there is just one explanatory variable—the growth rate. We now must relax this assumption and consider more than one explanatory variable. In practice there is almost always more than one explanatory variable. In the theory of voting behavior outlined in Chapter 1, for example, the vote share does not depend *only* on the growth rate. Other variables put forward were inflation, the number of good news quarters, whether the president is running for reelection, and a measure of duration. It is fortunately fairly easy to extend the analysis in this chapter to more than one explanatory variable. As an example, let's assume that the vote share depends on both the growth rate and inflation, as shown in Box 2-2.

BOX **2-2**

vote share depends on:	
	growth rate
	inflation

When there is more than one variable, we can no longer use a graph like Figure 2-1 to help us see what is going on. The line in Figure 2-1 is determined by two numbers, the intercept and the slope, but now we have three numbers to determine. From now on we will use the word *coefficient* instead of *slope* to refer to size of the effect associated with a variable. Using this terminology, the three numbers we have to determine in the present example are (1) the intercept, (2) the coefficient for the growth rate, and (3) the coefficient for inflation. Keep in mind that a coefficient is just a number, such as 0.9.

The line that fits the points best in Figure 2-1 is the one that has the smallest sum of squared errors. We imagined a computer trying thousands of lines, computing the sum of squared errors for each line, and choosing the line with the smallest sum. The line is characterized by a value for the intercept and a value for the slope (that is, a value for the coefficient for the growth rate).

For the present example, imagine the computer choosing three numbers: the intercept, the coefficient for the growth rate, and the coefficient for inflation. Given these three numbers, the computer can compute the error for each of the 21 elections. Consider, for example, the 1916 election, and assume that the three numbers are 51.0, 1.0, and -1.0. From Table 1-1 we see that the actual vote share for 1916 is 51.7, the growth rate is 2.2, and inflation is 4.3. Using the three numbers, the predicted vote share for 1916 is the intercept value of 51.0 plus 1.0 times the growth rate of 2.2 and -1.0 times inflation of 4.3. The predicted vote share is thus $51.0 + 2.2 - 4.3 = 48.9$. The error for 1916 is then the predicted value of 48.9 minus the actual value of 51.7, or -2.8. Using the same three numbers, the computer can compute the errors for the other 20 elections in the same manner. Each error is the difference between the predicted value for that election and the actual value. These predictions are after-the-fact predictions because they are based on the actual values of the growth rate and inflation. Once the 21 errors are computed, they can be squared and then summed.

We have seen so far that we can go from three numbers—the intercept, the coefficient for the growth rate, and the coefficient for inflation—to a value for the sum of squared errors. Now consider the computer doing this thousands of times, each time for a different set of three numbers, and in the end choosing the set of three numbers that has the smallest sum of squared errors associated with it. This best fitting set of three numbers is the analog of the best fitting line when there is only one explanatory variable.

Once the best fitting set of coefficients is found, we can compute the standard error. We first divide the sum of squared errors, which for our example turns out to be 406.3, by the number of observations (21) less the number of coefficients (3), or 18. This gives us 22.6. We then take the square root to get 4.8. The standard error (a measure of the size of a typical error) is thus 4.8.

The thought experiment that we used in Lesson 4 to derive the standard error of the estimated slope can be modified to incorporate more than one explanatory variable. For each set of 21 drawn errors (that is, for each universe), a best fitting set of coefficients is computed. After, say, 1,000 sets have been computed, a figure like Figure 2-3 can be drawn for each coefficient in the set. The standard error for a coefficient can then be determined by sweeping out 34.1 percent of the area as shown in Figure 2-3. The t-statistic for a coefficient is the coefficient divided by its standard error.

The results for the present example are:

BOX **2-3**

vote share depends on:		t-statistic
0.7	growth rate	3.1
−0.6	inflation	−1.6
54.2	intercept	26.3
standard error: 4.8		
number of observations: 21		

The coefficient for the growth rate is 0.7, with a t-statistic of 3.1. Since the t-statistic is greater than 2.0, it is unlikely that the true coefficient for the growth rate is zero. The growth rate is significant. The coefficient for inflation is −0.6, with a t-statistic of −1.6. The coefficient is negative, as the theory says, but the t-statistic is not less than −2.0. Inflation is thus not significant. This means that there is some nontrivial probability that the true coefficient for inflation is zero (that is, that inflation has no effect on the vote share). We will return to this result in the next chapter. The main point here is that it is possible to compute the coefficient and its associated t-statistic for each explanatory variable. There is nothing new in principle here from the case of just one explanatory variable.

Adding a third variable is also straightforward. There are then four coefficients to be computed instead of three, but all else remains the same. In practice it is quite easy for the computer to find the set of coefficients that leads to the smallest sum of squared errors. There are faster ways than the search procedure just discussed, but the answer is the same either way.

As a final point, we will sometimes use the phrase *other things being equal* in this book. This means we are engaging in the thought process of changing one explanatory variable without changing any of the others. For example, we might want to think about what happens to the vote share if the growth rate changes but inflation does not. We might then say that if the growth rate changes by such and such, the vote share will change by such and such, other things being equal. *Other things being equal* would mean that inflation does not change, nor does anything else that might affect the vote share.

Testing for Other Variables

We saw in the last section that each explanatory variable has associated with it a *t*-statistic. If the *t*-statistic for a particular variable is greater than 2.0 or less than −2.0, it is unlikely that the coefficient for the variable is zero. If the coefficient for the variable is not zero, then the variable has an effect on whatever is being explained, such as the vote share. It is thus easy to test whether a variable is supported by the data by including it in the fitting process and seeing if its *t*-statistic is greater than 2.0 or less than −2.0. This is a way of testing whether variables belong in the explanation (that is, whether variables are significant).

To give an example, say we are interested in whether the size of the armed forces affects the vote share. It may be that both the growth rate and the size of the armed forces affect the vote share. We can test for this by simply including the size of the armed forces along with the growth rate in the fitting process and seeing what the size of the *t*-statistic for the armed forces variable is.

Let's return now to possible pitfalls. Since it is so easy to try different variables or different sets of variables to see if they have large *t*-statistics, you can see why possible data mining is such a concern. Trying 100 combinations of variables and choosing the combination that leads to the best fit increases the chance that the chosen combination is spurious (that is, that it is just a fluke). Again, theory needs to be used to narrow the list of possible combinations.

We can now also be more precise about the problem of omitting the size of the armed forces from the explanation if it really belongs. If the growth rate tends to be high when the size of the armed forces is high and low when the size of the armed forces is low, and if both variables affect the vote share, then omitting the size of the armed forces will lead to a coefficient for the growth rate that is too large. For example, the 0.7 coefficient for the growth rate in Box 2-3 would be picking up the true effect of the growth rate on the vote share, which might be 0.5, and part of the effect of the size of the armed forces on the vote share, which might be 0.2. This would be an example of omitted variable bias, as mentioned in Lesson 5.

Horse Races

Many times in social science research we have two or more competing explanatory variables. It may be, for example, that it is not the growth rate that affects the vote share, but instead the change in the unemployment rate that does so. These two variables are strongly related, because when the growth rate is high the unemployment rate tends to decrease and vice versa. The two variables are not, however, perfectly related, and either variable is a plausible candidate for affecting votes for president.

It is fortunately easy to test between the growth rate and the change in the unemployment rate. We simply include both variables in the fitting process and compute the t-statistic for each. If one is significant (t-statistic larger than 2.0 or smaller than -2.0) and the other one is not, the one variable has dominated the other. We run, in other words, a *horse race* to see which variable dominates. We will perform a number of horse races in this book. A horse race is an effective way of allowing the data to choose which variable to keep. It may be, of course, that both variables are significant or that neither variable is significant. In these two cases the horse race is a tie (that is, the test is inconclusive).

Conclusion

We have covered a lot of material in this chapter, and if you have not seen any of it before, everything may not have sunk in completely. A good way to get an understanding of the tools is to see them in use, which is what the rest of this book is about. In the next chapter we test the theory of voting behavior outlined in Chapter 1. In the present chapter we simplified the theory to help in understanding the tools, but from now on we will cut no corners.

As we go through each chapter, keep in mind the seven lessons: proposing a theory, collecting data, fitting the data, using the data to test the theory, thinking about pitfalls, examining the results, and making a prediction.

3   Presidential Elections

How can I, that girl standing there,
My attention fix
On Roman or on Russian
Or on Spanish politics?
Yet here's a travelled man that knows
What he talks about,
And there's a politician
That has read and thought,
And maybe what they say is true
Of war and war's alarms,
But O that I were young again
And held her in my arms!

William Butler Yeats, Politics

The first draft of this chapter was written before the 2000 election. The last observation used for the fitting was the 1996 election. I have retained this time perspective in this chapter, which means that no information about the 2000 election has been used for any of the results. So as you read this chapter pretend that you don't know what happened in 2000. Chapter 4 then discusses how well the 2000 election was predicted, and it discusses predictions of the 2004 election.

A Theory of Voting Behavior

The theory of voting behavior that we are going to test is discussed in Chapter 1. We summarized the theory in Box 1-1, which is repeated on the next page.

The dependent variable is the vote share, and the explanatory variables are the other five variables in the box. Because we have already discussed this theory, we can move immediately to the data.

BOX **3-1**

vote share depends on:	
	growth rate
	inflation
	good news quarters
	president running
	duration

The Data

We are going to use the elections from 1916 to 1996 to test the theory. The relevant data are listed in Table 1-1, which was briefly discussed in Chapter 1. Since any test of a theory is no better than the data behind it, we need to be clear regarding the exact variables that were used. We will discuss each of the variables in turn. Refer back to Table 1-1 as the various variables are discussed.

The vote share that is used is the incumbent share of the two-party vote, not the incumbent share of the total vote. Which vote share should be used depends on who the third-party voters are. To take an example, assume that before a third-party candidate came along, 30 percent of the voters were staunch Republicans, 30 percent were staunch Democrats, and 40 percent were swing voters who were influenced by the economy. Assume also that the economy was neutral in the sense that half the swing voters were for the incumbent party and half were for the opposition party. In this case the vote share for the incumbent party would be 50 percent. This is, of course, both the total vote share and the two-party vote share, because there is no third party.

Now assume that a third-party candidate comes along and takes a third of the staunch Republicans, a third of the staunch Democrats, and none of the swing voters. Therefore, of all the voters, 20 percent are staunch Republicans, 20 percent are staunch Democrats, 20 percent are third-party voters, and 40 percent are swing voters. Assuming the economy is still neutral, half the swing voters vote for the incumbent party and half vote for the other main party. In this case the *total* vote share for the incumbent party is 40 percent (that is, 20 percent staunch voters plus 20 percent swing voters) out of the total of 100 percent. The *two-party* vote share for the incumbent party, on the other hand, is 50 percent (that is, 20 percent staunch voters plus 20 percent swing voters) out of the 80 percent two-party vote. The third-party candidate has thus lowered the total vote share for the incumbent party from 50 percent to 40 percent, but the two-party vote share remains the same at 50 percent. It is thus clear that a third-party candidate can affect the total vote share in a big way, but the effect on the two-party vote share may be modest, depending on how much the candidate takes from one party versus the other. By using the two-party vote share, we are in effect assuming that third-party candidates take about the same amount from each party.

The one exception to our use of the two-party vote share is the election of 1924. There is some evidence that La Follette (the third-party candidate, running for the Progressive Party) took more votes from Davis (the Democrat) than from Coolidge (the Republican). It has been estimated (see the notes to this chapter) that 76.5 percent of the votes for La Follette would otherwise have gone for Davis, with the remaining 23.5 percent going for Coolidge. The vote share for Coolidge was thus taken to be the number of votes that he got, plus 23.5 percent of the votes that La Follette got, divided by the total number of votes for all three.

The growth rate that is used is the growth rate in the first three quarters (nine months) of the election year. It is the *per capita* growth rate of real GDP, the growth rate of output per person. If the economy is growing only at the rate that population is growing, this is obviously less beneficial to the average person than if output per person is growing.

The measure of inflation is the average inflation rate over the 15 quarters prior to the election (that is, all the quarters of the administration except the last one). The variable used for inflation is the percentage change in the GDP deflator. As discussed in Chapter 1, inflation and deflation are treated symmetrically: deflation is assumed to be just as bad in voters' minds as inflation.

The *good news* variable is the number of quarters out of the 15 quarters before the election in which the growth rate exceeded 3.2 percent. (Remember, this is the *per capita* growth rate.) These are quarters in which the economy did exceptionally well, and the theory is that voters remember these kinds of events.

If the president is running for reelection, the *president running* variable is given a value of 1; otherwise the value is 0. Vice presidents who became president during the administration were given a 1 if they ran again, except for Ford. Ford was given a 0 because he was not on the elected ticket but was appointed vice president when Agnew resigned.

The *duration* variable, which is listed in Table 1-1, is given a value of 0.0 if the incumbent party has been in office for only one consecutive term, 1.0 for two consecutive terms, 1.25 for three consecutive terms, 1.5 for four consecutive terms, and 1.75 for five consecutive terms.

This completes the discussion of the variables in Box 3-1, but there are two other variables that need to be mentioned. First, a *party* variable was included that has a value of 1 if the incumbent party is Democratic and -1 if the incumbent party is Republican. This variable tests whether there is a pure party effect (that is, whether there is a tendency for voters to favor one party over the other). Second, the elections of 1920, 1944, and 1948 were treated somewhat differently because of the wars. The period prior to the 1920 election was dominated by World War I, and the periods prior to the 1944 and 1948 elections were dominated by World War II. The inflation variable and the good news variable were assumed not to be relevant for these three elections. In other words, voters were assumed not to take into account past inflation and good news when deciding how to vote during the three war-dominated periods. This treatment requires that a *war* variable be included that has a value of 1 for the 1920, 1944, and 1948 elections and a value of 0 otherwise. It also means that the values used for the inflation and good news variables for these three elections are 0, not the values listed in Table 1-1.

Fit and Test and Examine

We are now ready to see how well the explanatory variables do in explaining the vote share. Their coefficients are determined in the manner discussed in the last chapter. The set of coefficients is found that results in the smallest sum of squared errors, and the *t*-statistics are computed. The data used are from Table 1-1. The results are shown in Box 3-2.

BOX **3-2**

vote share depends on:		t-statistic
0.70	growth rate	7.46
−0.71	inflation	−2.75
0.90	good news quarters	3.84
4.0	president running	3.23
−3.3	duration	−3.06
−2.8	party variable	−5.16
4.7	war variable	1.98
48.4	intercept	19.02
standard error: 2.2		
number of observations: 21		

In this case there were eight coefficients to determine, one for each of the eight variables in the box (counting the intercept). There are thus eight corresponding t-statistics.

It will be convenient after considering how well we have fit the data to discuss the size of the coefficients at the same time as we discuss their t-statistics. If we were exactly following the lessons in Chapter 2, we would not discuss the size of the coefficients until Saturday, after we had discussed the t-statistics and thought about possible pitfalls. Only if the t-statistics look good and the possible pitfalls seem minor should we care about the coefficients. We will be jumping ahead only for convenience of discussion.

Let's begin with the standard error in the box, which is 2.2. A typical error is thus 2.2, which is fairly small. As discussed in the last chapter, we know that 68.2 percent of the time the error in predicting the vote share will be between −2.2 and 2.2.

We can get a more detailed picture of the errors by looking at Table 3-1. The table shows, for each of the 21 elections, the actual vote share, the predicted vote share, and the error (predicted minus actual). The predictions in this table are after-the-fact predictions. This means that the actual values of the explanatory variables were used for the predictions. For each election, each coefficient in Box 3-2 was multiplied by

TABLE **3-1** Actual and Predicted Vote Share

Year	In Power	Election Outcome	Actual Vote Share (%)	Predicted Vote Share (%)	Predicted Minus Actual (%)
1916	D	President Wilson beat Hughes	51.7	50.7	−1.0
1920	D	Cox lost to Harding	36.1	38.9	2.8
1924	R	President Coolidge beat Davis and La Follette	58.2	57.8	−0.4
1928	R	Hoover beat Smith	58.8	57.3	−1.5
1932	R	President Hoover lost to F. Roosevelt	40.8	39.1	−1.7
1936	D	President F. Roosevelt beat Landon	62.5	64.3	1.8
1940	D	President F. Roosevelt beat Willkie	55.0	56.0	1.0
1944	D	President F. Roosevelt beat Dewey	53.8	52.9	−0.9
1948	D	President Truman beat Dewey	52.4	50.5	−1.9
1952	D	Stevenson lost to Eisenhower	44.6	43.9	−0.7
1956	R	President Eisenhower beat Stevenson	57.8	57.3	−0.5
1960	R	Nixon lost to Kennedy	49.9	51.1	1.2
1964	D	President Johnson beat Goldwater	61.3	61.3	0.0
1968	D	Humphrey lost to Nixon	49.6	49.6	0.0
1972	R	President Nixon beat McGovern	61.8	59.8	−2.0
1976	R	Ford lost to Carter	48.9	48.6	−0.3
1980	D	President Carter lost to Reagan	44.7	45.6	0.9
1984	R	President Reagan beat Mondale	59.2	61.5	2.3
1988	R	G. Bush beat Dukakis	53.9	52.4	−1.5
1992	R	President G. Bush lost to Clinton	46.5	50.9	4.4
1996	D	President Clinton beat Dole	54.7	52.6	−2.1

the actual value of the respective variable for that coefficient, with the answers then being added to get the predicted value for that election. If this is not completely clear, we will go over this procedure in more detail in the next chapter. You may also want to review the discussion of after-the-fact predictions at the end of Lesson 7 in Chapter 2.

The largest error in Table 3-1 is for the 1992 election, where President George Bush got 46.5 percent of the vote and was predicted to get 50.9 percent, an error of 4.4. The next largest error is for the 1920 election, where Cox got 36.1 percent and was predicted to get 38.9 percent, an error of 2.8. Then comes the 1984 election, where President Reagan got 59.2 percent and was predicted to get 61.5 percent, an error of 2.3. All the remaining errors are between −2.1 and 1.8.

The winners of two elections were predicted incorrectly: 1960 and 1992. In 1960 Nixon got 49.9 percent of the vote, a loss, but was

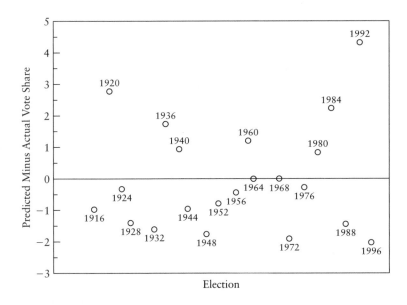

FIGURE **3-1** **Predicted Minus Actual Vote Share**

predicted to get 51.1 percent, a win, which is an error of 1.2. Even though the winner was predicted incorrectly, the error was small, so in this sense the election was predicted well. In 1992 President Bush got 46.5 percent of the vote, a loss, but was predicted to get 50.9 percent, a win, which is an error of 4.4. In this case the winner was predicted incorrectly, and the error was large.

For those who like pictures, Figure 3-1 plots the last column of Table 3-1. The errors are plotted for each election, starting from the earliest. The large positive error for 1992 stands out in the figure.

Having examined the errors, let's now turn to the coefficients and their associated *t*-statistics. The coefficient for the growth rate is 0.70, which says that if the growth rate increases by 1.0, the vote share is predicted to increase by 0.70. The coefficient for inflation is −0.71, which says that if inflation increases by 1.0, the vote share is predicted to decrease by 0.71. The growth rate and inflation thus have similar effects on the vote share except that one effect is positive and the other is negative. The *t*-statistic for the growth rate is 7.46, and since this value is considerably greater than 2.0, it is highly unlikely that the true coefficient for the growth rate is zero. In other words, it is quite likely that the growth rate affects the vote share. The t-statistic for inflation is -2.75, and since this value is less than -2.0, it is unlikely that the coefficient for inflation is zero. In other words, it is likely that inflation affects the vote share. The growth rate and inflation are thus both significant.

The coefficient for the good news variable is 0.90, which means that each additional good news quarter is predicted to increase the vote share by 0.90. This is a fairly large effect. The t-statistic for the good news variable is 3.84, so it also unlikely that the true coefficient for the good news variable is zero.

The coefficient for the president running variable is 4.0, which means that a president running for another term is predicted to have a head start of 4.0 percentage points. The t-statistic is 3.23, so it is unlikely that the true coefficient is zero. If the true coefficient were zero, the president running would have no head start.

The duration variable has a coefficient of -3.3 with a t-statistic of -3.06. If a party has been in power for two consecutive terms, it is predicted to start out behind by 3.3 percentage points, because the duration variable has a value of 1.0 in this case. If a party has been in power for three consecutive terms, it is predicted to start out behind by $3.3 \times 1.25 = 4.125$ percentage points, because the duration variable has a value of 1.25 in this case. For four consecutive terms the value is $3.3 \times 1.50 = 4.95$ percentage points, and so on. The duration variable is significant because its t-statistic is less than -2.0.

The coefficient for the party variable is -2.8 with a t-statistic of -5.16. Since the t-statistic is much less than -2.0, it is highly unlikely that the true coefficient for the party variable is zero. Remember that the party variable has a value of 1 for the Democrats and -1 for the Republicans. The coefficient thus says that when the incumbent party is Democratic, it is predicted to start out behind by 2.8 percentage points and when the incumbent party is Republican, it is predicted to start out ahead by 2.8 percentage points. There is thus a tendency for voters to favor Republicans, other things being equal.

The coefficient for the war variable is only relevant for three elections. Its t-statistic is 1.98. Although the t-statistic is not quite 2.0, the cutoff we are using for calling a variable significant, it is still fairly unlikely that the true coefficient is zero. The variable is thus "almost" significant.

Overall, the results seem very good. The errors are small except for 1992, and the t-statistics are all greater than 2.0 or less than -2.0, with one slight exception. In particular, the t-statistics for the economic variables (the growth rate, inflation, and the number of good news quarters) suggest that the economy does have an effect on the vote share; it is very unlikely that we would get these t-statistics if the economy did not affect the vote share. We cannot, however, relax, because of the possible pitfalls lurking in the background. To this we now turn.

Possible Pitfalls

The main pitfall that we need to worry about is the possibility of data mining. Many variables were tried in arriving at the final results, and we have only 21 observations. It may be that by chance we have fit the data well but that in fact the vote share is determined by other things. The following are the main things that were tried that may be subject to the data mining problem.

- Increments other than 0.25 were tried for the duration variable, and 0.25 was chosen because it gave the best results in terms of fit.
- Values other than 3.2 percent were tried for the cutoff for the good news variable, and 3.2 was chosen because it gave the best results in terms of fit.
- The particular treatment for the wars for the three elections was done because this led to an improved fit.
- Different periods for the growth rate were tried, and the particular one chosen, the first three quarters of the election year, gave the best results in terms of fit.
- Different periods for inflation were also tried, and the particular one chosen, the entire four-year period except for the last quarter, gave the best results in terms of fit.
- After the large error was made in 1992, an attempt was made to find reasons for it. This effort led to the choice of the good news variable, which prior to 1992 had not been thought of.

The good news variable helps make the error for 1992 smaller because, as you can see from Table 1-1, there was only one good news quarter for the Bush administration. President Bush is still predicted to win in 1992 in Table 3-1, but by less than he would be predicted to if it were not for the good news variable.

With only 21 elections and all this searching, it is certainly possible that the results in Box 3-2 are a fluke and are not really right. As discussed in Chapter 2, one way of examining the seriousness of the data mining problem is to see how well future observations are predicted. If the results are a fluke, future predictions should not in general be very accurate. In particular, if the results are a fluke, the prediction for the 2000 election is not likely to be accurate, since no information about that election was used in getting the results. The prediction of the 2000 election is discussed in the next chapter.

An alternative approach to examining the data mining problem is to use only part of the observations to get the coefficients and then see how well these coefficients do in predicting the other observations. This is not as good a check as waiting, because we have used information in the whole sample (both parts) to decide which variables to include, but at least the coefficients are obtained using only the information in the first part of the observations.

To perform this check, the best fitting set of coefficients was obtained using only the elections through 1960. In other words, the best fit was obtained for the 1916–1960 period (12 elections), with no data from 1964 or later being used. The best fitting coefficients for this set of observations are shown in Box 3-3.

These coefficients obviously differ from the earlier ones because they are based on only 12 observations rather than 21. The coefficient for the growth rate still has a large t-statistic, and its value has changed only slightly—from 0.70 to 0.83. The t-statistic for the inflation coefficient, however, is now only -1.15. The inflation coefficient has changed from -0.71 to -0.42. The results are thus weak for inflation affecting the vote share if the observations we use stop in 1960.

Perhaps the most important result is that the t-statistic for the good news variable is still fairly large (2.64). Even though the good news variable was not formulated until after the 1992 election, its

BOX **3-3**

vote share depends on:		*t*-statistic
0.83	growth rate	7.75
−0.42	inflation	−1.15
0.66	good news quarters	2.64
5.3	president running	4.25
−1.8	duration	−1.97
−3.7	party variable	−6.15
4.2	war variable	1.78
47.3	intercept	21.10
standard error: 1.5		
number of observations: 12		

significance does not depend on the 1992 observation. Even stopping in 1960, the results say that a zero coefficient for the good news variable is unlikely. The size of the coefficient has fallen from 0.90 to 0.66, although it is still significant.

We can use this new set of coefficients to predict the outcomes of elections after 1960. These predictions are presented in Table 3-2. These are after-the-fact predictions, as are the ones in Table 3-1. The predictions in the two tables differ because they are based on the use of different coefficients. If data mining is a serious problem, the predictions in Table 3-2 should generally not be very good because the coefficients have been estimated using only data through 1960.

The predictions in Table 3-2 are in fact fairly good. The only very large error is for 1992, where it is 8.5. The next largest error is for 1984, where President Reagan got 59.2 percent of the vote and was predicted to get 63.1 percent, an error of 3.9. Otherwise, the errors are between −2.4 and 2.7. Remember that by the 1996 election the prediction is based on a set of coefficients that was chosen using data ending 36 years earlier!

This analysis thus suggests that data mining may not be a serious problem, but one can never be sure. The results need to be interpreted with some caution. This is particularly true in light of the large error for

TABLE **3-2** **Actual and Predicted Vote Share—1960 Coefficients**

Year	In Power	Election Outcome	Actual Vote Share (%)	Predicted Vote Share (%)	Predicted Minus Actual (%)
1964	D	President Johnson beat Goldwater	61.3	59.2	−2.1
1968	D	Humphrey lost to Nixon	49.6	49.0	−0.6
1972	R	President Nixon beat McGovern	61.8	62.1	0.3
1976	R	Ford lost to Carter	48.9	51.6	2.7
1980	D	President Carter lost to Reagan	44.7	45.6	0.9
1984	R	President Reagan beat Mondale	59.2	63.1	3.9
1988	R	G. Bush beat Dukakis	53.9	53.4	−0.5
1992	R	President G. Bush lost to Clinton	46.5	55.0	8.5
1996	D	President Clinton beat Dole	54.7	52.3	−2.4

1992. It may be that 1992 is just an unusual draw—something unlikely to happen very often—but it could also signal a permanent change in the relationship between the economic variables and the vote share. To know this, we simply have to wait for more elections. It is encouraging that the 1996 election was predicted fairly well, since if there has been a permanent change in the relationship we would expect a large error in 1996. (We will also see in the next chapter that the 2000 election was predicted very well.)

What About the Electoral College?

Nothing has been said so far about the electoral college. The dependent variable (that is, the variable to be explained) has been taken to be the incumbent party's share of the two-party vote, not the party's share in the electoral college. A candidate could get less than 50 percent of the two-party vote and yet get more than 50 percent of the electoral college votes, thus winning the election. This happened in 1876 (Hayes versus Tilden) and in 1888 (Harrison versus Cleveland). (It also happened in 2000, but this is material for the next chapter.)

The aim of our analysis is to explain voting behavior in the sense of explaining how many votes one party gets relative to the other in the whole country. The aim is not to explain how many states go for one party over the other.

Nor is the aim of the analysis to explain who wins the election. The theory is judged by how close the predicted values of the two-party vote share are to the actual values (that is, by the size of the errors). Consider two hypothetical elections in which the incumbent party is the Democratic Party and in which it wins both times. Say the party's vote share is 61 percent in the first election and 51 percent in the second. Say also that the predicted vote share is 54 percent for the first election and 49 percent for the second. The winner was thus correctly predicted for the first election, but the error was fairly large at -7 percentage points; much of the large margin for the Democrats was not predicted. On the other hand, the winner was incorrectly predicted for the second election, but the error was small at 2 percentage points; the election was predicted to be close, and it was. The second election is thus predicted better than the first, even though the winner was predicted incorrectly in the second. As a social scientist trying to explain the vote share, I care about the size of my errors, not about who wins. This point is not always easy to get across to reporters, and I sometimes sound uncaring.

Do Campaigns Matter?

Nothing has been said about campaigns. Does this mean that campaigns don't matter, that all that matters are the incumbency information and the economic variables? What if one party campaigned and the other did not? Wouldn't this make a difference? This is a commonly asked question, especially by those considering working on a campaign. A related question that is sometimes asked is whether it matters who is nominated. What if some extreme left- or right-wing candidate were nominated? Wouldn't this have a big effect on the outcome?

The answer is that campaigns are likely to matter and that the nomination of an extreme candidate is likely to make a difference. This does not, however, call into question the above analysis, and the reason is somewhat subtle to grasp. Remember what is being explained—the voting that actually takes place on election day. It seems safe to say that in all 21 elections both parties campaigned hard. Each party did its best, given the issues, and so forth. Each of the 21 vote shares is thus based on strong campaigns by both parties. In none of the 21 elections did one party not campaign, so our analysis has nothing to say about what would happen if one party did not campaign. We are asking the question of what determines the vote share *given* that both parties campaign hard (which they always do).

Similarly, extremists do not get nominated by the two parties (yes, I know, some will disagree with this statement), so our analysis has nothing to say about what would happen if a party nominated one. Again, we are asking the question of what determines the vote share, *given* that both parties nominate nonextremists.

To take one more example, say that two months before an election some new campaign tactic of one of the parties, such as negative ads, appears to be working well. The other party is likely to counter with its own negative ads, and in the end the new tactics of the two parties would probably roughly cancel each other out. Again, each party has done its best by election time, and we are looking at voting behavior after all the hard campaigning has been done.

Manipulating the Economy to Increase Votes

As previously discussed, different periods for the growth rate were tried, and the period that led to the best results in terms of fit was the first three quarters of the election year. The growth rates in the earlier quarters matter in that they can contribute to the number of good news quarters, but they do not get extra weight beyond this. Voters appear to give the more recent experience more weight—"recent" in this case being the election year. This weighting is consistent with a number of psychological experiments, where what happens at the end of an experiment is remembered more than what happens otherwise (see the note to Chapter 1).

Because a strong growth rate in the year of the election is good for the incumbent party, there is an incentive for the incumbent party to try to stimulate the economy in the election year to help get reelected. One strategy would be to slow the economy in the middle of the four-year term and then stimulate hard in the final year and a half or so. Slowing the economy in the middle of the term would allow more room for rapid growth at the end. If this were done, there would be a four-year business cycle in which the trough would be reached near the middle of the four-year period and the peak would be reached near the end.

This type of business cycle is called a *political business cycle*. The cycle is political in that it is induced by the incumbent party manipulating the economy for its own political purpose.

Whether this strategy has been pursued at some points in the past (that is, whether there are in fact political business cycles) is hard to test. There are four-year periods in which a trough was reached in the middle and a peak came at the end, but it is hard do know if this were done deliberately by the party in power. There is also the question whether an administration has the ability to manipulate the economy in such a precise way, especially if the other party has control of Congress. It may be that some have tried and failed. This question of how parties behave regarding the economy once in power is not the same as the question of how voters behave, and we have only been concerned in this chapter with the behavior of voters.

Does Congress Matter?

An implicit assumption behind our theory of voting behavior is that voters praise or blame the White House for the state of the economy, not the Congress. If one party controls the White House and the other controls the Congress, who should be judged? The above theory is obviously wrong if the answer is Congress, and this is another possible pitfall that should be kept in mind. Casual observation suggests that the buck stops at the White House, but we have simply assumed this to be true and have not tested it.

Do Voters Really Know the Growth Rate and Inflation Numbers?

I have often been asked if I really believe that many voters know the actual values of the growth rate and inflation when they enter the voting booth on election day. How many people really look up the numbers in their newspapers before voting? (This is usually a hostile question.) It is surely unlikely that many voters know the exact numbers. They form their opinions about the economy by looking at the conditions around them—how their friends and neighbors and employers are doing—not by looking at the numbers themselves. They may also be influenced by the media, especially radio and television commentators. The numbers, however, are likely to be related to the conditions that people are observing. If the growth rate is negative, for example, it is likely that the conditions that people see around them are not so good and that commentators are saying bad things about the economy. It is thus not necessary that voters know the exact numbers as long as the numbers accurately reflect what the voters are actually paying attention to.

4   Predicting the 2000 and 2004 Elections

All secrets of earth are known to Zeus and Apollo;
But of mortal prophets, that one knows more than another
No man can surely say; wisdom is given
To all in their several degrees.

> *Sophocles, from* King Oedipus

The 2000 election was close and exciting. Al Gore got 50.3 percent of the two-party vote, but he lost the election in the electoral college after Florida was declared a win for George W. Bush. As exciting as the end game in Florida was, it is not our concern here. We are interested in explaining voting behavior as measured by the share of the two-party vote. On this measure the election was essentially a tie, and from the point of view of testing the theory it does not really matter who won. Our main concern here is whether the theory predicted a close election or not. A prediction of a close election is evidence in favor of the theory; conversely, a prediction of a large margin of victory is evidence against the theory.

After-the-Fact Prediction of the 2000 Election

To give some reinforcement on what is involved in making a prediction, we will go through the process of predicting the 2000 election step by step. We begin with the coefficients in Box 3-2. These coefficients were estimated using data on the 21 elections between 1916 and 1996. We discussed in Chapter 3 how after-the-fact predictions are made. For a given election we multiply each coefficient by the actual value of its variable, then add up the results to get the predicted value. We did this in the last chapter for the elections only through 1996. Now we are ready to make an after-the-fact prediction of the 2000 election.

At the time of this writing (November 2001) data for 2000 are available for all the variables we need. Box 4-1 lists the calculations that are needed to make a forecast for 2000.

BOX **4-1**

After-the-Fact Prediction for 2000			
coefficient	value	coefficient × value	
0.70	2.2	1.5	growth rate
−0.71	1.7	−1.2	inflation
0.90	7	6.4	good news quarters
4.0	0.0	0.0	president running
−3.3	1.0	−3.3	duration
−2.8	1.0	−2.8	party variable
4.7	0.0	0.0	war variable
48.4	1.0	48.4	intercept
		49.0	TOTAL (vote share)

President Clinton did not run, so the president running variable has a value of 0.0. The duration value is 1.0 because the Democratic Party had been in power for two consecutive terms. The Democratic Party was the incumbent party in 2000, so the party variable has a value of 1.0. The value of the war variable is 0.0. All this, of course, was known way ahead of the election. After the fact, we now know the values of the economic variables. The value of the growth rate was 2.2 percent, inflation was 1.7 percent, and the number of good news quarters was 7. Given these values, the predicted value of the Democratic Party vote share for 2000 can be computed, as shown in the box. The third column shows the result of multiplying each coefficient by the value of its variable. The last line of the column is the sum of all the items in the column. The sum is the predicted vote share for the Democrats, which is 49.0 percent.

How accurate is the prediction of 49.0 percent? It is in fact quite accurate. As noted above, Gore got 50.3 percent of the two-party vote, so the error is only −1.3, less than the standard error, as reported in Box 3-2, of 2.2. The error for 2000 is thus well within what one would expect if the theory is true, so the results for 2000 are consistent with the theory. The election was very close, and it was predicted to be very close.

We can see from Box 4-1 why the election was predicted to be close. On the negative side for the Democrats, the party variable and the duration variable took away votes. The party variable always works against the Democrats. In addition, in 2000 the Democrats had been in power for two consecutive terms, so the duration variable was also working against them. You can see in the box that the party variable contributes -2.8 and the duration variable contributes -3.3. Also, the president himself was not running, so there was no positive president running effect. The president running value in the box is 0.0. On the positive side for the Democrats, the economy was moderately good. The growth rate was a modest 2.2 percent, inflation was low at 1.7 percent, and the number of good news quarters was 7, which is slightly above average (see Table 1-1 for the data through 1996). In the box the growth rate contributes 1.5, inflation takes away 1.2, and the number of good news quarters contributes 6.4. The net effect of this is that the election was predicted to be close. The economy would have had to have been stronger (say a 5 percent growth rate and 10 good news quarters) in order for the prediction to have been strongly in favor of the Democrats.

The small error for 2000 is encouraging regarding the possible data mining problem. If this problem is serious and the results in the last chapter are essentially a fluke, the 2000 election should not in general have been predicted well because the 2000 data were not used in the search for the best fit. The small error is thus evidence against data mining, although this is, of course, only one new observation.

Real-Time Predictions of the 2000 Election

The coefficients in Box 3-2 were estimated in November 1998. The actual values of the economic variables for the 2000 election were not, of course, known at that time, but predictions of those variables were available from various sources. Given predictions of the economic variables, we can use the coefficients to make a prediction of the vote share, just as we did in the previous section using the actual values of the economic variables. Remember that predictions that are based on

TABLE **4-1** Predictions of the 2000 Vote Share (Actual Vote Share Was 50.3%)

| Date of Prediction | Predicted Economic Values | | | Vote Shares (%) | |
	Growth Rate (%)	Inflation Rate (%)	Good News Quarters	Predicted	Predicted Minus Actual
Real-Time Predictions					
November 6, 1998	0.9	1.4	3	44.7	−5.6
January 30, 1999	1.1	1.4	4	45.7	−4.6
May 1, 1999	1.7	1.5	6	47.9	−2.4
November 5, 1999	2.2	1.8	5	47.1	−3.2
January 29, 2000	2.1	1.8	6	47.9	−2.4
April 28, 2000	3.8	2.0	8	50.8	0.5
July 31, 2000	3.6	1.8	8	50.8	0.5
October 27, 2000	3.5	1.7	8	50.8	0.5
After-the-Fact Prediction					
	Actual Economic Values:				
July 27, 2001	2.2	1.7	7	49.0	−1.3

predicted as opposed to actual values of the explanatory variables are called *real-time* predictions.

Between November 6, 1998, and October 27, 2000, I made eight real-time predictions of the vote share for 2000, all using the coefficients in Box 3-2. The predictions of the economic variables were from my economic model of the United States. Table 4-1 presents these eight real-time vote share predictions, along with the after-the-fact prediction discussed in the previous section.

The first prediction was made on November 6, 1998, two years ahead of the election. It was based on values of 0.9 percent for the growth rate, 1.4 percent for inflation, and 3 for the number of good news quarters. The predicted vote share for the Democrats was 44.7 percent. Since the actual vote share for the Democrats turned out to be 50.3 percent, this is an error of −5.6. This was thus not a very accurate forecast. The inaccuracy of the prediction is not, however, a criticism of the theory. We know that the error is only −1.3 when the actual values of the economic variables are used, the values that should be used when testing the theory. The large real-time error in November 1998 was due to the use of values for the growth rate and the number of good news quarters that were too low. In other words, the economy turned out to be stronger than a 0.9 percent growth rate and 3 good news quarters. The use of these low values resulted in a prediction of the Democratic vote share that was much too low.

The predictions of the growth rate and the number of good news quarters tended to get larger over time, so the predicted vote share tended to get larger. By May 1, 1999, the election was beginning to be predicted to be close, with a predicted vote share of 47.9 percent. By April 28, 2000, the election was predicted to be very close, with a predicted vote share of 50.8 percent. The last three real-time predictions in Table 4-1 were based on values of the growth rate and the number of good news quarters that were somewhat too high, which is the reason the three vote share predictions (all 50.8) are slightly higher than the after-the-fact prediction (49.0).

Aside from the first two real-time predictions in Table 4-1, the predictions were on average quite accurate. The last three were especially accurate, with an error of only 0.5. Remember that the predictions prior to July 31, 2000, were made before the candidates were even known! These three predictions are more accurate than predictions made in late August 2000 at the American Political Science Association meeting in Washington, D.C. Six of the seven predictions at this meeting had Gore getting between 52.3 and 55.4 percent of the two-party vote, and the seventh had Gore getting 60.3 percent (R. Kaiser, "Political Scientists: Gore is the Winner," *Washington Post,* August 31, 2000). The last three predictions in Table 4-1 are even more accurate than the polls in the last few days, which had Gore getting about 48 percent of the two-party vote.

So as a real-time prediction device, the use of the economic predictions in Table 4-1 and the coefficients in Box 3-2 gave quite accurate predictions of the 2000 election. Beginning about a year and a half ahead, and especially in the last six months, the election was predicted to be close.

Real-Time Predictions of the 2004 Election Using the 1996 Coefficients

I hope I have whetted your appetite for real-time predictions of the 2004 election, given that the real-time predictions of the 2000

election were so good. It is easy to use the coefficients in Box 3-2 to predict 2004. We need, of course, economic predictions for 2004 first.

Although we need economic predictions before we make a vote
share prediction, we can say something interesting before considering the
economic predictions. Let's assume that President Bush runs for reelection in 2004. We know from Box 3-2 that this gives him 4.0 percentage
points. In addition, the Republican Party is the incumbent party, giving it
2.8 percentage points. The Republican Party will have been in office only
one consecutive term, so there is no duration penalty. This is the best possible incumbency situation: a Republican president running for reelection
when the Republicans have been in power for only one term. President
Bush is thus predicted to begin with a large head start.

To digress briefly, it is interesting to see what has happened in this
incumbency situation before. If you turn back to Table 1-1, you can see
that there are four cases in which a Republican president ran for reelection
when the Republican Party had been in power only one term. In 1984 President Reagan beat Mondale with 59.2 percent of the vote, in 1972 President Nixon beat McGovern with 61.8 percent of the vote, in 1956
President Eisenhower beat Stevenson with 57.8 percent of the vote, and in
1924 President Coolidge beat Davis with 58.2 percent of the vote. These
are all very large victories.

Let's now return to 2004. At the time of this writing (November
2001), it is known that the economy started the year slowly for the Bush
administration and that it was hurt by the terrorist attacks of September 11, 2001. There have been no good news quarters yet. Many expect
that a recovery will begin in early 2002, but this is far from certain. The
following box shows the prediction calculations using a growth rate of
1.5 percent, inflation of 3.0 percent, and 3 good news quarters. (Remember that the growth rate pertains to the first three quarters of 2004.) These
are modest economic values. The calculations are shown in Box 4-2.

You can see that President Bush is predicted to get 56.9 percent of
the two-party vote, a fairly large victory. In other words, because of the
favorable incumbency situation, President Bush is predicted to win fairly
easily even if economic growth is only modest.

What would it take for President Bush to be predicted to lose?
If the number of good news quarters is 1 rather than 3, this takes
away 1.8 percentage points because each good news quarter contributes

BOX **4-2**

Real-Time Prediction for 2004			
coefficient	value	coefficient × value	
0.70	1.5	1.1	growth rate
−0.71	3.0	−2.1	inflation
0.90	3	2.7	good news quarters
4.0	1.0	4.0	president running
−3.3	0.0	0.0	duration
−2.8	−1.0	2.8	party variable
4.7	0.0	0.0	war variable
48.4	1.0	48.4	intercept
		56.9	TOTAL (vote share)

0.90 percentage points. (From Table 1-1 you can see that President Bush's father had only 1 good news quarter during his administration.) If inflation is 5.5 percent rather than 3.0 percent, say because of a large oil price shock, this takes away 1.8 percentage points because each percentage point of inflation takes away 0.71 percentage points. If the growth rate is −3.5 percent rather than 1.5 percent, this takes away 3.5 percentage points because each percentage point of growth rate adds 0.70 percentage points. The total loss is thus 7.1 percentage points (1.8 + 1.8 + 3.5), which gives President Bush 49.8 percent of the two-party vote.

You can thus see that the economy would have to be quite weak before President Bush would be predicted to lose. Remember, however, that the standard error is 2.2 percentage points (that is, the average error that has been made historically). This means that even if President Bush were predicted to get, say, 52.0 percent of the vote, there is still a nontrivial chance that the error would be larger than 2.0 and thus that he would lose (at least in the popular vote).

How much confidence should you place on this conclusion that President Bush will be hard to beat in 2004? This is where the possible pitfalls take center stage. What about data mining? Even though the election of 2000 was predicted well, maybe this was a fluke and Box 3-2 is not in fact an accurate explanation of voting behavior. In particular, maybe the predicted 4.0 head start for President Bush because he is running again is too large, having been influenced too much by the four cases mentioned above where a Republican president ran for reelection when the Republican Party had been in power for only one term. Or maybe voting behavior will change in 2004, so that Box 3-2 is only of historical interest. Maybe voters will change their focus from economic matters to social and international concerns and turn away from the Republican Party's policies.

You should thus take all this with considerable caution. Possible pitfalls are always with us. The election of 2004 will be an important test of the theory. A strong conclusion has been drawn, namely that President Bush will be very hard to beat, and if the error for 2004 turns out to be small, the theory will have done very well. (Remember, I am speaking only as a social scientist here. This says nothing about my political views.) If, on the other hand, the economy is good and President Bush loses, this will be a large error and will not be supportive of the theory as represented in Box 3-2.

Real-Time Predictions of the 2004 Election Using the 2000 Coefficients

In the previous section we used the coefficients in Box 3-2, which are estimated using data from 1916 through 1996, to make the 2004 prediction. Now that the observation for 2000 is available, new coefficients can be estimated using data from 1916 through 2000. In other words, all the results in Chapter 3 can be updated through the 2000 election. Once this is done, the new coefficients can be used to predict the 2004 election. I will do this updating in November 2002, and these results will be posted on my Web site: http://fairmodel.econ.yale.edu. It is unlikely, however, that the new coefficients will differ much from the ones in Box 3-2. The error for 2000 was small, and in this sense there are no surprises in the extra observation. If there were only one explanatory variable, we could say that the 2000 observation is almost on the line in Figure 2-1, so the position of the best fitting line is not likely to change much when we add 2000 to the sample period. The general conclusion reached in the previous section about President Bush's chances is thus not likely to be changed by the updating.

5   Extramarital Affairs

The heavens rejoyce in motion, why should I
Abjure my so much lov'd variety,
And not with many youth and love divide?
Pleasure is none, if not diversifi'd.

John Donne, Elegie XVII, Variety

We now move from politics to sex, two areas that are sometimes related. Politics and sex are actually related in two ways. One obvious way is that some politicians, including a recent president, engage in extramarital affairs (and sometimes get caught!) The other way is that both how people vote and whether they engage in extramarital affairs are aspects of human behavior that social scientists can attempt to explain. Just as we asked what factors influence how someone votes, we can ask what factors lead someone to have an affair.

Many people engage in extramarital affairs. Most of us probably have at least one friend who we know is having an affair or who has had one in the past. A question a social scientist might ask is, what motivates people to have affairs? Just as we examined voting behavior in the last chapter, we can examine affair behavior. In this chapter we examine the question of what affects a person's behavior regarding the amount of time spent (if any) in an affair.

We begin as usual with a theory—a theory of affair behavior. We next discuss the data that were used to test the theory, and then we test it. Once we have finished with the tests, we can use the results to predict the amount of time (if any) a person with certain characteristics will spend in an affair.

Although this topic may seem unusual for a social scientist to examine, affairs are an important part of many people's lives, and it is of interest to see if any of this behavior can be explained. The topic provides another good example of how the tools in Chapter 2 can be used.

A Theory of Extramarital Affairs

The primary motivation for the theory is the idea that people like variety in their lives. This idea is hardly novel or controversial, and it is easy to find defenses for it. They range from the cliché "variety is the spice of life" to the poem of John Donne at the beginning of this chapter. We will apply this idea to leisure activities, one of which is the amount of time spent in an affair.

We begin with the concept of *utility,* which is commonly used in economics to mean satisfaction or happiness. My son gets utility from going to a baseball game. I get utility from running and from watching *Antiques Roadshow.* As with satisfaction or happiness, the more utility the better. *Disutility* is negative utility. If we are doing something we don't like to do, we are said to be getting disutility from it.

We proceed with the theory by considering a married woman, Lynn, and assuming that she can engage in three types of activities: time spent with spouse, time spent with paramour, and time working. (Lynn could be a man: just change *she* to *he* and *her* to *his* in the following discussion.) In the marriage Lynn gets utility from time spent with her spouse and from the amount of goods consumed with her spouse. In the affair Lynn gets utility from time spent with her paramour and from the amount of goods consumed with her paramour. Lynn receives two types of income. First, her parents left her a trust fund that gives her a certain amount of money each month, independent of how much she works. This is called her *nonwage income.* Second, she works, and her *wage income* is her wage rate times the number of hours that she works. She uses both of her incomes to buy goods for the marriage and for the affair. The more she works, the more income she has to buy goods.

What is Lynn free to decide? There are about 720 hours in a month. She can decide how many of these hours to spend with her spouse, with her paramour, and at work. The total number of hours cannot, of course, exceed the total number of hours in the month. Given the prices of the goods, she also decides how many goods to buy for the marriage and how many for the affair. The total amount that she spends on goods cannot exceed the sum of her nonwage and wage income. (We are assuming no borrowing and no taxes.)

Lynn is assumed to make her decisions so that she receives the largest possible total utility (that is, the utility from the marriage *plus* the utility from the affair). This assumption of utility maximization is common in economics. People are assumed to behave by making themselves as happy or satisfied as possible. (This assumption drives some social scientists nuts—but this is another story.) Lynn is thus assumed to maximize total utility, subject to the constraints that her nonwage and wage income cannot exceed her purchases of goods and that the more she works, the less time she has to spend in the marriage and the affair.

We can now consider an important implication of the theory that Lynn behaves by maximizing total utility. What happens if Lynn's aunt dies and leaves her with a second trust, one from which she receives a certain amount of money each month? Her nonwage income rises. Assume that nothing else has changed. Lynn is better off, and when she remaximizes with this higher income, she increases the four things that give her positive utility: time spent with spouse, time spent with paramour, goods consumed in the marriage, and goods consumed in the affair. She works less because she is spending more time in the marriage and the affair. So time spent with paramour will increase when nonwage income increases. We will call this an *income effect*.

What happens if instead Lynn's wage rate increases? You might at first think that the same thing would happen, namely, that she would increase the four things that give her utility, including time spent with paramour. The fact that this may not happen illustrates one of the key insights of economics. This insight concerns the difference between an *income effect* and a *substitution effect*. Say that Lynn's wage rate has doubled, from $20 per hour to $40 per hour. Because the reward from working has gone up, Lynn has an incentive to do more of it. Before, when Lynn thought about working an extra hour, she knew she could buy $20 more in goods for the hour worked; now she can buy double that amount. Lynn thus has an incentive to work more because of the extra reward. If she works more, she has less time to spend in the marriage and the affair, so these times will fall. Lynn has "substituted" her time away from the marriage and the affair into work.

There is also, however, something else going on in this case. For any given number of hours worked, Lynn makes more than she did before. Say Lynn worked 160 hours a month before the change, so her wage income was $3,200 a month. If she still worked this amount after her wage rate doubled, her wage income would be $6,400 a month. Her income is thus higher for the same number of hours worked, and we know that, other things being equal, higher income leads her to increase the four things that give her positive utility, including time spent in the marriage and in the affair. If she spends more time with her spouse and with her paramour, she spends less time working. If we focus only on this effect, she will work less than she did before (that is, less than 160 hours a month).

So what can we say about the effects of an increase in Lynn's wage rate on the amount of time she spends in the affair? We don't know. Lynn is better off because, for a given number of hours worked, she has more income. This alone would lead her to increase all four things. She would buy more goods and spend more time in the marriage and in the affair (and thus also work less). She can both work less and buy more goods because she is making more per hour worked. On the other hand, each hour of work is now more lucrative, and this alone would lead her to work more. If she works more, she spends less time in the marriage and the affair. The income effect is thus leading her to work less, and the substitution effect is leading her to work more, and the net effect could go either way. If the income effect dominates, she spends less time working and more time in the affair, and if the substitution effect dominates, she spends more time working and less time in the affair.

The key economic insight here is that people may respond differently to an increase in nonwage income than to an increase in the wage rate. A nonwage income increase, such as extra money each month from a trust fund, does not change the amount received for an additional hour worked, so there is no substitution incentive. There is thus no substitution effect when nonwage income increases, and such an increase has the effect of decreasing the time spent working. People who win big in the lottery usually work less afterward than they otherwise would have. When the wage rate increases, on the other hand, there are both income and substitution effects; with the income effect leading to less work and the substitution effect leading to more, the net effect could go either way. People may or may not work less when their wage rate increases.

The income effect and the substitution effect are the two main economic implications of the theory. There are obviously also noneconomic factors at work, and these will be discussed as we present the data. Anything that has a positive effect on the utility from the marriage leads to less time spent in the affair. Conversely, anything that has a positive effect on the utility from the affair leads to more time spent in the affair.

A person may choose to spend no time in an affair. If Lynn receives no utility (or even negative utility) from an affair under any circumstance, she will spend no time in one. In this case a change in, say, Lynn's nonwage income will not affect her time spent in an affair, since affair activity never gives her positive utility. The theory does not require that a person spend time in an affair. If a person is having an affair, the theory is concerned with variables that affect the amount of time spent in the affair, but none of these variables matter if a person never receives positive utility from an affair.

The Data

As you might suspect, it is not easy to find data to test the theory. The government, for example, does not collect data on extramarital affair activity. The data that were found are from two magazine surveys. The first survey was conducted in 1969 by *Psychology Today (PT)*. A questionnaire on sexual activity was published in the July 1969 issue of *PT,* and readers were asked to mail in their answers. About 20,000 replies were received, of which about 2,000 were coded onto tape. (For young readers: data used to be stored on magnetic tapes for distribution; now data are stored on CDs.) The second survey, for women only, was conducted in 1974 by *Redbook (RB)*. A questionnaire on sexual activity was published in the October 1974 issue of *RB*, and readers were asked to mail in their answers. About 100,000 replies were received, of which about 18,000 were coded onto tape. The questionnaires included questions about extramarital affairs as well as about many other aspects of sexual behavior and about various demographic and economic characteristics of the individual.

Table 5-1 lists the variables that were constructed from the data on the two tapes. Only people who were currently married and who had been married only once were included from each tape. People who had

TABLE **5-1** Data for Testing the Theory of Extramarital Affairs

Variable	Description	Values	Mean
	Psychology Today Data		
affair	How often engaged in extramarital sexual intercourse during the past year	0 = none, 1 = once, 2 = twice, 3 = 3 times, 7 = 4–10 times, 12 = monthly, 12 = weekly, 12 = daily	1.46
years married	Number of years married	0.125 = 3 months or less, 0.417 = 4–6 months, 0.75 = 6 months–1 year, 1.5 = 1–2 years, 4 = 3–5 years, 7 = 6–8 years, 10 = 9–11 years, 15 = 12 or more years	8.18
age	Age	17.5 = under 20, 22 = 20–24, 27 = 25–29, 32 = 30–34, 37 = 35–39, 42 = 40–44, 47 = 45–49, 52 = 50–54, 57 = 55 or over	32.50
marital happiness	Rating of marriage	5 = very happy, 4 = happier than average, 3 = average, 2 = some-what unhappy, 1 = very unhappy	3.93
religiosity	Rating of how religious	5 = very, 4 = somewhat, 3 = slightly, 2 = not at all, 1 = anti	3.12
occupation	Occupation	Values between 1 and 7, ranked by social position of occupation	4.19
	Redbook Data (women only)		
affair	Measure of time spent in extramarital affairs	Equal to 0 if no sexual relations with man other than husband; otherwise equal to (no. men × frequency)/years married. (Values range from 0 to 57.6.)	0.705
no. men	If since marriage have had sexual relations with man other than husband, with how many different men	1 = 1, 3.5 = 2–5, 8 = 6–10, 12 = more than 10	N/A

TABLE **5-1** continued

Variable	Description	Values	Mean
	Redbook Data (women only)		
frequency	Continuing from previous question, approximate number of times had sexual relations with each man	1 = once, 3.5 = 2–5, 8 = 6–10, 12 = more than 10, 5.6 = it varied greatly from partner to partner	N/A
years married	Number of years married	0.5 = less than 1 year, 2.5 = 1–4 years, 6 = 5–7 years, 9 = 8–10 years, 13 if more than 10 years and oldest child is under 12 years of age, 16.5 if more than 10 years and oldest child is between 12 and 17 years of age, 23 if more than 10 years and oldest child is 18 years of age or over	9.01
age	Age	17.5 = under 20, 22 = 20–24, 27 = 25–29, 32 = 30–34, 37 = 35–39, 42 = 40 or over	29.1
marital happiness	Rating of marriage	5 = very good, 4 = good, 3 = fair, 2 = poor, 1 = very poor	4.11
religiosity	Rating of how religious	4 = strongly, 3 = fairly, 2 = mildly, 1 = not	2.43
occupation	Occupation	6 = professional with advanced degree; 5 = managerial, administrative, business; 4 = teacher, counselor, social worker, nurse, artist, writer; technician, skilled worker; 3 = white-collar (sales, clerical, secretarial), 2 = farming, agriculture, semiskilled or unskilled worker, other; 1 = student	3.42

Note: *Psychology Today* data consist of 601 observations, 150 of them where affair is not zero. *Redbook* data consist of 6,366 observations, 2,053 of them where affair is not zero.

been married more than once were excluded because of lack of information on some of the variables for these people. In particular, the question regarding the number of years the person has been married pertains to all marriages; if a person has been married more than once, the length of the current marriage cannot be determined. Also, only people who were employed were included from each tape. Unemployed people were excluded because the theory does not necessarily pertain to them. The theory pertains to people deciding how much time to work versus how much time to spend doing other things, and people who are not working at all are a special case and are to some extent outside of the theory. Also, excluded from the tapes were people who failed to answer all the relevant questions.

After these exclusions, there were 601 observations left from the *PT* tape. Of these, 150 (25.0 percent) had at least one affair during the past year. There were 6,366 observations left from the *RB* tape. Of these, 2,053 (32.2 percent) had at least one affair since the person's marriage.

Table 5-1 lists each variable and how it was constructed. In the Values column, the items to the right of the equals sign are the answers that were allowed on the questionnaires. The numbers to the left of the equals signs are the values that I chose to represent the answer. A number of questions were open-ended in the upper range, and in each of these cases I had to make a fairly arbitrary choice for the largest value of the variable.

The *RB* questionnaire did not ask if the person was currently having an affair. The affair variable that was used in this case was taken to be the number of different men with whom the woman had had sexual relations since the marriage times the frequency with each man and then this divided by the number of years married. This affair variable is at least a rough measure of the time spent in extramarital affairs.

The one economic variable from each tape is occupation. Each occupation is assigned a number based primarily on social position—the larger the number, the higher the social position. We will use this variable as a proxy for the person's wage rate, but it is at best a rough approximation. The ranking of jobs by social position is not exactly the same as the ranking of jobs by the size of the wage rate, so the occupation variable is not a perfect measure of the person's wage rate. It is, unfortunately, all we have.

We will test the theory by estimating coefficients for the variables as shown in Box 5-1.

BOX **5-1**

affair depends on:	
	occupation
	years married
	age
	marital happiness
	religiosity

What does the theory say about these variables? If we assume that occupation is a proxy for a person's wage rate, then the theory says that occupation is likely to have an effect on the affair variable, but whether the effect is positive or negative is ambiguous. If the income effect dominates, the effect is positive, and if the substitution effect dominates, the effect is negative.

If the number of years married has a negative effect on the utility from the marriage because of boredom, then the variable years married should have a positive effect on affair. Remember that the individual (Lynn) is maximizing total utility—the utility from the marriage plus the utility from the affair—and if utility from the marriage is low because of boredom, total utility will be maximized by spending more time in the affair than otherwise.

If age has a negative effect on the enjoyment of sexual activity, something that may or may not be true (see Chapter 8 for estimates of how fast people slow down), and if affairs are primarily sexual, then age will have a negative effect on the utility from the affair. If the utility from the affair is low because of small sexual pleasure, total utility will be maximized by spending less time in the affair than otherwise.

If marital happiness has a positive effect on the utility from the marriage (which seems obvious), then it should have a negative effect on affair. For a happily married person, total utility will be maximized by spending more time in the marriage than otherwise.

If a person's religious intensity has a negative effect on the utility from the affair, then the variable religiosity should have a negative effect on the affair. A religious person may be concerned about possible divine disapprobation from engaging in an affair, and he or she may not feel good about having one, or at least about spending much time in one.

Fit and Test

We are now ready to estimate the coefficients and their t-statistics. Once again, we tell the computer to find the set of coefficients that gives the best fit—the smallest sum of squared errors. The one new wrinkle concerns the large number of zero values for the affair variable. If someone is not having an affair, he or she may not be close to starting one. (As discussed above, the person may receive no utility from an affair under any circumstance.) For this person a decrease in, say, religious intensity is unlikely to lead the person to begin an affair. This is in contrast to someone who is already having an affair, where a decrease in religious intensity may lead the person to spend at least a little more time in the affair.

There are thus, to some extent, two types of people: those who are unlikely to be moved from zero by at least modest changes in the explanatory variables, and those who are not at zero and may change the amount of time in the affair as the explanatory variables change. We thus need to account for the fact that things are different when the value of the dependent variable is zero than when it is above zero. There are methods that take into account this difference, and I have used one of these methods here. It is still the case that a type of best fit is obtained. It is just that the measure of how well a set of coefficients fits the data is not exactly the sum of the squared errors. The insights from Chapter 2, however, are still relevant. (It is beyond the scope of this book to discuss this method.)

The results for the two surveys are shown in Boxes 5-2 and 5-3. Let's look at the occupation variable first. It has a positive coefficient in both cases. It is significant for the *Redbook* data, but it has a t-statistic of only 1.29 for the *Psychology Today* data. The results are thus mixed, but there is at least some evidence that occupation has a positive effect on an affair. To the extent that the occupation variable is a proxy for the wage rate, the positive effect means that the income effect dominates the substitution effect. A high wage person relative to a low wage person, other things equal, works less and spends more time in an affair.

The other coefficients have the expected sign and are significant. The number of years married has a positive effect on affair (the boredom effect), and age has a negative effect (the physical slowing down effect). Marital happiness has a negative effect, as expected, and the religiosity variable has a negative effect, again as expected if there is a fear of divine disapprobation by religious people.

BOX **5-2**

Psychology Today data		
affair depends on:		t-statistic
0.326	occupation	1.29
0.554	years married	4.13
−0.179	age	−2.26
−2.28	marital happiness	−5.61
−1.69	religiosity	−4.14
8.17	intercept	2.96
standard error: 2.87		
number of observations: 601		

BOX **5-3**

Redbook data		
affair depends on:		t-statistic
0.255	occupation	3.30
0.140	years married	6.11
−0.120	age	−4.91
−1.53	marital happiness	−20.82
−0.950	religiosity	−11.14
7.18	intercept	11.39
standard error: 2.12		
number of observations: 6,366		

As with many studies in social science, the testing of the present theory is limited by the quality of the data. An important test of the theory would be to have a measure of nonwage income. The theory says that nonwage income should have an unambiguously positive effect on time spent in the affair. Unfortunately, we have no such variable to include, and this aspect of the theory cannot be tested.

Data exist on the level of education of the person and the number of children in the marriage. These two variables were added, and neither was significant for either data set. The lack of significance of the education variable is perhaps not surprising, since there is no particular reason to expect that the level of education of a person affects the utility from the marriage and the utility from the affair differently. On the other hand, one might expect the number of children to increase the utility from the marriage and thus for the number of children to have a negative effect on time spent in the affair. Since the number of children was not significant in either data set, there is no evidence that this is true. Children seem to be a wash, at least in these two data sets.

Possible Pitfalls

As discussed in the previous section, the lack of data on nonwage income limits the testing of the economic implications of the theory. Also, the occupation variable is at best only a crude measure of a person's wage rate. Better tests could be made with better data. The quality of the data is something that you should keep in mind in deciding how much to trust the current results.

The rest of this section is hard, and it can be skipped if desired. It concerns an important and difficult problem that arises in social science research: *selection bias*. It will take some time to explain what this means. We will take a simple example to illustrate the point. We will assume that the time spent in an affair depends only on marital happiness. Figure 5-1 is a graph of hypothetical data, with time spent in an affair on the vertical axis and marital happiness on the horizontal axis. Let's also forget the zero problem and assume that everyone is spending at least a little time in an affair. (Selection bias can exist with or without any zeros.)

Figure 5-1 shows the best fitting line using all the points in the figure. There are a number of points for people with a marital happiness value of 5, a number for those with a value of 4, and similarly for values of 3, 2, and 1. The line is downward sloping: the happier one is in the marriage, the smaller the amount of time spent in the affair.

Let's first consider what is *not* a problem. It is all right if we do not have a random sample of the population regarding the degree of marital happiness. Say that our sample contains a much larger fraction of unhappily married people than is true in the total population. (Perhaps *Psychology Today* and *Redbook* readers are on average less happily

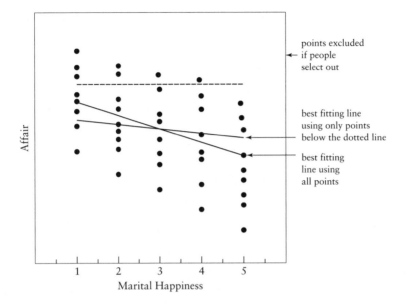

FIGURE **5-1**   **Example of Selection Bias**

married than is the total population.) All this means regarding Figure 5-1 is that we have an unrepresentatively large number of points for marital happiness of 1 and 2 and an unrepresentatively small number of points for marital happiness of 4 and 5. There is, however, no bias when we find the best fitting line using our data. Just because we have a relatively large number of observations for a particular happiness level does not mean that the points that we have are on average too high or too low. Remember that the distance from a point to the line is an *error*. In the present context an error reflects all the things that affect time spent in an affair aside from marital happiness. For any sample of people of, say, happiness level 4, some are above the line and some are below the line, but there is no reason to think that more are above than below. You can think about the errors for these people as being drawn randomly from a bell-shaped curve like that in Figure 2-2. Nothing that was said in Chapter 2 requires that we have a representative sample. It thus does not matter that the *Psychology Today* and *Redbook* readers are unlikely to be representative samples of the total population regarding variables like marital happiness (that is, the explanatory variables).

So what is the selection bias problem? This problem occurs if people choose to answer the questionnaire based on how much time they are spending in an affair. It may be, for example, that people who spend little time in an affair don't find the questionnaire as interesting and are thus less inclined to fill it out than those who are quite active in an affair. Or it may be the case that people who are quite active in an affair are less inclined to fill out the questionnaire for fear of arousing suspicion from a possibly already suspicious spouse. In either case our estimate of the slope will be wrong (biased).

To take a specific example, consider all the points above the dotted line in Figure 5-1. These are people who spend considerable time in an affair. You can see that more of the points occur for people who have a low marital happiness rating (1 or 2) than for those who have a high rating (4 or 5). This, of course, is as expected. We are much less likely to find a happily married person spending a large amount of time in an affair than we are to find an unhappily married person spending a large amount of time in one. Another way of looking at this is that the error for a happily married person spending a large amount of time in an affair is large, and large errors are less likely to be drawn from a bell-shaped curve than are small ones.

Now let's say that no one above the dotted line fills out the questionnaire for fear of getting caught. When we collect the data, we thus see only the points below the dotted line. What happens when we find the best fitting line using only the points below the dotted line? It should not be surprising that the slope of the line changes. In this case, the slope would get flatter, as shown in Figure 5-1. We have excluded more high points around happiness levels 1 and 2 than around 4 and 5, and this distorts the best fitting line. The slope is wrong, or biased. This in a nutshell is the selection bias problem.

To summarize, the selection bias problem arises when the choice of whether a person participates in a study depends on the size of the dependent variable.

Is selection bias likely to be a problem in the *PT* and *RB* data? As previously discussed, one can tell plausible sounding stories in both directions—people who are very active selecting out and people who are very inactive selecting out. This is to some extent good, since there is no strong argument for one side only. There is no real way of knowing, however, so selection bias is another possible pitfall that you must keep in the back of your mind when judging the results.

One last point on the sample. We discussed above why it is not a problem if the *Psychology Today* and *Redbook* readers are not a representative sample of the total population as long as there is no selection bias. When we say this, however, we are assuming that the coefficients are the same for everyone in the population. People can differ in the values of the explanatory variables, but not in the coefficients that are attached to these variables. If the coefficients differ among individuals, we are in a different ball game. If coefficients differ across groups of individuals, such as *Psychology Today* and *Redbook* readers versus *Field and Stream* readers, we must treat each group separately in the sense of finding the best fitting set of coefficients, group by group. We cannot combine the groups and find the best fitting set of coefficients, because no such set exists.

Examine the Results and Predict

To the extent we can trust the results, how can we use them? The results say that the amount of time spent in an affair depends positively on the person's occupation (wage rate) and number of years married. It depends negatively on the person's age, marital happiness, and religious intensity. We can thus say that if we know someone who (1) has a high wage rate, (2) has been married a long time, (3) is fairly young given the length of time he or she has been married, (4) is unhappily married, and (5) is not religious, then this person is a likely candidate for spending considerable time in an affair. We can thus get from the results a sense of who is and who is not likely to have an active affair life.

We can also make quantitative statements using the size of the coefficients. The following numbers are approximately correct for people who are already spending time in an affair and are not close to the margin of ending the affair (see the notes to this chapter for more details). The numbers are not accurate for people who are not currently in an affair or are in an affair but are close to the margin of ending it.

Let us consider the *PT* results first. If the number of years married increases by 10 years, the affair variable increases by 5.54 (the coefficient of 0.554 times 10). An extra 10 years of marriage thus increases the number of sexual encounters per year by between 5 and 6. On the other hand, an increase in a person's age by 10 years decreases the number of encounters by 1.79, or about 2 per year. If marital happiness decreases from happier than average (rating 4) to somewhat unhappy (2), the number of encounters increases by 4.56, or between 4 and 5 times a year. If the religiosity variable decreases from somewhat (rating 4) to not at all (2), the number of encounters increases by 3.38, or about 3 times per year.

We can do the same thing for the *RB* results. An extra 10 years of marriage leads to an increase of 1.4 encounters per year. An extra 10 years of age leads to a decrease of 1.2 encounters per year. A 2 point drop in marital happiness leads to an increase of 3.06 encounters per year. A 2 point drop in religiosity leads to an increase of 1.9 encounters per year.

These kinds of statements are, of course, of limited interest because there is no specific person we are talking about. They do, however, give you a sense of magnitudes.

Conclusion

How many chapters on sex have you read where you learned about income and substitution effects as well as selection bias, not to mention the use of interesting statistical tools? But enough of sex and lemans; we are now on to wine.

6   Wine Quality

A cup of wine that's brisk and fine,
And drink unto the leman mine;
And a merry heart lives long-a

William Shakespeare, from King Henry IV, Part II

This is a chapter that will make some wine connoisseurs mad. We will show that the tools in Chapter 2 can be used to explain and predict wine quality. Some people feel that wine quality is too subtle to be quantified. How can a social scientist, who may not know a Bordeaux from a Burgundy, explain and predict wine quality better than wine experts? This chapter shows how. It is based on a fascinating (to me at least) article by Orley Ashenfelter, David Ashmore, and Robert Lalonde, "Bordeaux Wine Vintage Quality and the Weather," *Chance* (1995), 7–14. (I am indebted to the authors for supplying me with their data.)

In what follows, *vintage* means the year in which the wine was bottled and *wine quality* means the quality the wine ultimately attains after it has properly aged. Keep in mind that the quality a wine ultimately attains is not known with certainty at the time it is bottled. Generally young wines don't taste very good, and it takes years to know for sure how good the wine is.

We will deal in this chapter with red Bordeaux wines from the top châteaux (vineyards). There is nothing in the following analysis, however, that prevents the procedure from being used for other types of wines.

Theory and Data

The theory is simple. It is that wine quality depends on the weather in the harvest year. The best conditions are when (1) the growing season

(April–September) is warm, (2) August and September are dry, and (3) the previous winter (October–March) has been wet. This is a theory that most people, including wine experts, accept. Casual observation reveals that the great Bordeaux vintages have corresponded to warm growing seasons, dry Augusts and Septembers, and previous wet winters.

You should now have had enough experience from the previous chapters to see where we might go with this. If we can get a measure of wine quality and if we can get measures of the weather in the Bordeaux region of France, we can use the weather variables to help explain the wine quality variable.

The first step is to get a measure of wine quality. In 1855 the châteaux in the Médoc region of Bordeaux were ranked by quality and put into five classes, with the top châteaux receiving a *premier cru* rating. This ranking was based on the price of the wine. Châteaux with the highest prices for their wines were given the *premier cru* rating; châteaux with slightly lower prices were given the next ranking (*second cru*); and so on. Using prices to measure quality seems perfectly sensible. The better a wine, the higher we would expect its price to be.

We will deal with six châteaux. The ranking of these six using today's prices is Latour, Lafite, Cheval Blanc, Pichon-Lalande, Cos d'Estournel, and Montrose. The 1855 classification of these wines has held up fairly well over time. The ranking in 1855 was Lafite, Latour, Pichon-Lalande, Cos d'Estournel, and Montrose (Cheval Blanc was not ranked in 1855). Latour and Lafite were ranked *premier cru* in 1855, and Pichon-Lalande, Cos d'Estournel, and Montrose were ranked *second cru*.

The reason wine quality varies across châteaux has to do with the geography of the vineyard. The best wines are produced on a slope with a southern exposure to the sun and in soil with good drainage. Although it is interesting to compare wines of the same vintage across châteaux, such as comparing a 1966 Latour to a 1966 Montrose, this is not the subject matter of this chapter. (As just noted, differences across châteaux primarily reflect differences in the geography of the vineyards.) We are instead interested in the prices of different vintages from the same château. How does, say, a 1961 Lafite compare to a 1963 Lafite? The above theory says that this difference should depend on the weather in 1961 versus that in 1963.

Wines trade in secondary (auction) markets, with one of the main markets located in London, so it is possible to get data on prices of wines by château and vintage from these markets. We can, for example, get the price of a 1961 Lafite, a 1962 Lafite, a 1961 Latour, a 1962 Latour, and so on. Since we are interested in different years, one possibility for a price variable would simply be to take a particular château, say Latour, and use the prices of the Latour vintages. The price variable actually used, however, is a weighted average of the prices of the six châteaux listed above. For example, the price used for the 1966 vintage is a weighted average of the six châteaux's prices for the 1966 vintage. By not relying solely on one château, this procedure probably gives slightly better estimates of the price differences across vintage years. The six châteaux were chosen because they are large producers and their wines appear frequently in the auction markets. The prices were the ones recorded in London in 1990–91.

Regarding the weather variables, data on Bordeaux's weather are readily available from historical records. Three measures of weather have been used: (1) the average temperature in April–September, (2) the amount of rainfall in August and September, and (3) the amount of rainfall in the preceding October–March period.

The theory is that vintage price depends on the three weather variables. One other variable is also likely to matter, which is the age of the vintage. It costs money to store wines, so, other things being equal, older wines should sell for more than younger ones to compensate people for the extra holding period.

The theory is summarized in Box 6-1.

BOX **6-1**

vintage price depends on:		
	temperature April–Sept.	
	rainfall Aug.–Sept.	
	rainfall previous Oct.–March	
	age of vintage	

The data are presented in Table 6-1. The vintage years are from 1952 through 1980, with 1954 and 1956 excluded because of insufficient

TABLE **6-1** Data for Explaining Wine Prices

Vintage	Price (1961 = 1.000)	Temp Average April–Sept. (°C)	Total Rainfall Aug.–Sept. (ml)	Rainfall Previous Oct.–March (ml)	Age (1983 = 0)
1952	0.368	17.12	160	600	31
1953	0.635	16.73	80	690	30
1955	0.446	17.15	130	502	28
1957	0.221	16.13	110	420	26
1958	0.180	16.42	187	582	25
1959	0.658	17.48	187	485	24
1960	0.139	16.42	290	763	23
1961	1.000	17.33	38	830	22
1962	0.331	16.30	52	697	21
1963	0.168	15.72	155	608	20
1964	0.306	17.27	96	402	19
1965	0.106	15.37	267	602	18
1966	0.473	16.53	86	819	17
1967	0.191	16.23	118	714	16
1968	0.105	16.20	292	610	15
1969	0.117	16.55	244	575	14
1970	0.404	16.67	89	622	13
1971	0.272	16.77	112	551	12
1972	0.101	14.98	158	536	11
1973	0.156	17.07	123	376	10
1974	0.111	16.30	184	574	9
1975	0.301	16.95	171	572	8
1976	0.253	17.65	247	418	7
1977	0.107	15.58	87	821	6
1978	0.270	15.82	51	763	5
1979	0.214	16.17	122	717	4
1980	0.136	16.00	74	578	3

data. (By 1990, the 1954 and 1956 vintages were no longer traded much; they were not very good.) There are thus 27 observations. The table lists the price variable, the three weather variables, and the vintage age variable. The price variable is the price of the vintage relative to the price of the 1961 vintage. The 1966 price of 0.473, for example, means that the 1966 vintage sold for 47.3 percent of the 1961 vintage.

The 1961 vintage was truly outstanding—the best of the 27 vintages in Table 6-1 in terms of price. You can see that the weather was excellent in 1961. The temperature in April–September was very warm

(17.33 degrees centigrade), there was almost no rainfall in August–September (38 milliliters), and there was considerable rainfall the previous October–March (830 milliliters). It doesn't get much better than this. A real dog was 1968, with a fairly cold growing season (16.20 degrees centigrade), considerable rainfall in August–September (292 milliliters), and modest rainfall the previous winter (610 milliliters). The price of the 1968 vintage is only 10.5 percent of the 1961 vintage price!

You may examine Table 6-1 for more examples if you wish, but our concern now is to find the set of coefficients that best explains the price. This is done in the next section.

Fit the Data

The dependent variable is the vintage price, and the explanatory variables are the four variables in Box 6-1 plus the intercept. The procedure is the same as in Chapter 2: we find the best fitting set of coefficients and then compute the t-statistics. The vintage price variable that is used for these calculations is expressed in percentage terms. (To be more precise, the price variable used is the logarithm of the price variable in Table 6-1, although it is not really necessary to know this. The main point is that the price variable used in the estimation is in percentage terms.) The results are presented in Box 6-2.

The three weather variables are significant and have the expected signs, so there is support for the theory. The temperature in

BOX **6-2**

vintage price depends on:		t-statistic
.617	temperature April–Sept.	6.49
−.00387	rainfall Aug.–Sept.	−4.80
.00117	rainfall previous Oct.–March	2.43
.0239	age of vintage	3.34
−12.16	intercept	−7.21
standard error: 0.286		
number of observations: 27		

April–September has a positive coefficient and a t-statistic of 6.49. Rainfall in August–September has a negative coefficient and a t-statistic of −4.80. And rainfall in the previous October–March has a positive coefficient and a t-statistic of 2.43. The vintage age variable is also significant. The coefficient of .0239 says that, other things being equal, a vintage price rises 2.39 percent per year.

To see how well the vintage price has been explained, we have listed the predicted and actual values in Table 6-2 for each of the 27 vintage years. The predicted values in Table 6-2 are after-the-fact predicted values, which means that the actual values of the weather variables have been used for the predictions. Table 6-2 is similar to Table 3-2, which

TABLE **6-2** Actual Versus Predicted Wine Prices by Vintage

Vintage	Actual Price (1961 = 1.000)	Predicted Price	Percentage Error
1952	0.368	0.463	0.229
1953	0.635	0.538	−0.166
1955	0.446	0.439	−0.015
1957	0.221	0.219	−0.009
1958	0.180	0.230	0.243
1959	0.658	0.385	−0.536
1960	0.139	0.182	0.268
1961	1.000	0.891	−0.115
1962	0.331	0.374	0.121
1963	0.168	0.154	−0.085
1964	0.306	0.387	0.235
1965	0.106	0.076	−0.328
1966	0.473	0.396	−0.178
1967	0.191	0.251	0.273
1968	0.105	0.109	0.034
1969	0.117	0.152	0.263
1970	0.404	0.308	−0.272
1971	0.272	0.269	−0.011
1972	0.101	0.072	−0.344
1973	0.156	0.241	0.435
1974	0.111	0.146	0.272
1975	0.301	0.223	−0.300
1976	0.253	0.209	−0.192
1977	0.107	0.169	0.457
1978	0.270	0.206	−0.273
1979	0.214	0.179	−0.177
1980	0.136	0.161	0.171

listed the predicted and actual values of the vote share. The vintage price variable that is used in Table 6-2 is the same as the one in Table 6-1. It is the ratio of each vintage price to the 1961 vintage price. Each error in the table is the percentage error. For example, for 1952 the actual price is 0.368, the predicted price is 0.463, and the percentage error is 0.229 (22.9 percent). (To be precise, the percentage error is the logarithm of the predicted price minus the logarithm of the actual price, but it is not necessary to know this.) Note that the standard error from Box 6-2 is 0.286 (28.6 percent), which means that on average we should see an error of roughly that size.

The largest error in the table is for 1959. The actual price is 0.658, which is quite high, but the predicted price is only 0.385. The percentage error is −0.536, over a −50 percent error. You can see from Table 6-1 that in 1959 the April–September temperature was quite warm, which is good, but there was a lot of rain in August–September and less rain than average the previous October–March, both of which are not good. The net effect is that the 1959 vintage is not predicted to be nearly as good as it was.

There are two errors larger than 40 percent in Table 6-2. These are 43.5 percent for 1973 and 45.7 percent for 1977. Each of these vintages is low priced. The percentage errors are graphed in Figure 6-1, where you can easily see these two errors.

Overall, the results seem fairly good. The three weather variables are significant, and their coefficient estimates are of the expected signs. The standard error is 0.286, so that about 68 percent of the time we can expect an error in predicting the price between −28.6 and 28.6 percent.

Possible Pitfalls

Probably the main possible pitfall is that the weather variables may be too simple to capture adequately the subtle effects of the weather on wine quality. Only three variables are used for the entire year, and possibly more are needed. The authors of this study did try a fourth weather variable, the average temperature in September of the harvest year, but it was not significant. It still may be, however, that other measures of the weather would improve the fit (that is, lower the standard error).

There is also the possibility of data mining. If the authors tried many weather variables and picked the three that gave the best fit, the

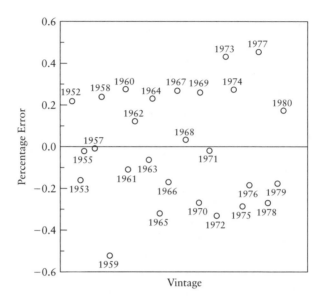

FIGURE **6-1** Percentage Errors Predicting Wine Prices

results may be a fluke. In other words, the three weather variables may fit the data well for the particular 27 vintage years but may not in fact capture well the ways in which weather affects wine quality. We will do a test for this in the next section.

Another potentially serious pitfall is that prices may not accurately reflect quality. If a particular wine becomes "hot" for some faddish reason that has nothing to do with the quality of the wine, its price may rise far above what its true quality would dictate. In other words, there could be conspicuous consumption effects on wine prices independent of quality. There is currently, for example, a very influential wine critic, Robert Parker, whose views on wines seem to affect their prices. If Parker is sometimes wrong about a wine's quality (no one is perfect) and if his ratings affect prices, then a wine's price may deviate from its true quality. We will have more to say about this issue in the next section, where an alternative measure of quality is discussed.

I said at the beginning of this chapter that using statistical tools to predict wine quality would make some wine connoisseurs mad. Can three weather variables really do all the work? You know now, of course, that fits are not perfect in the sense that generally there are errors. The weather variables clearly cannot do all the work, and we have seen that the standard error is 28.6 percent. Some people don't understand about errors of this sort, and an amusing example of this is a comment that occurred in the magazine *Wine Spectator* on the authors' attempt to explain wine quality.

> The theory depends for its persuasiveness on the match between vintage quality as predicted by climate data, and vintage price on the auction market. But the predictions come out exactly true only 3 times in the 27 vintages since 1961 that he's calculated, even though the formula was specifically designed to fit price data that already existed. The predicted prices are both under and over the actual prices.

(The vintages actually begin in 1952, not 1961.) As my children would say, duh!

Predict

An interesting test of the theory is to use the coefficients in Box 6-2 to predict vintage prices beyond 1980, the last vintage in the sample. Let's focus on five vintages: 1987, 1988, 1989, 1990, and 1991. Table 6-3 presents data on the three weather variables for each of these vintages. The age variable is also included in the table. The age variable is taken to be 0 in 1983 (see Table 6-1), so its values for 1987 and beyond are negative. The age variable is a counting variable, and it does not matter which year is taken to be 0. All that matters is that the variable change by 1 each year, which it does.

TABLE **6-3** Data for Predicting Wine Prices, 1987–1991

Vintage	Temp. April–Sept. (°C)	Total Rainfall Aug.–Sept. (ml)	Rainfall Previous Oct.–March (ml)	Age (1983 = 0)
1987	16.98	115	452	−4
1988	17.10	59	808	−5
1989	18.60	82	443	−6
1990	18.70	80	468	−7
1991	17.70	183	570	−8

TABLE **6-4** Predicted Wine Prices by Vintage, 1987–1991

Vintage	Predicted Price (1961 = 1.000)
1987	.184
1988	.364
1989	.536
1990	.578
1991	.231

We can use the values of the weather variables and the coefficients in Box 6-2 to predict the vintage price for each of the five years. These are after-the-fact predictions because they are based on actual values of the explanatory variables, although they use only coefficients that have been estimated from data up to 1980. If data mining is a serious problem, these predictions should not generally be very good because the 1987–91 observations have not been used in getting the coefficients. In fact, the predictions are 8 to 12 years past the last year of the sample.

The predictions are presented in Table 6-4. You can see that the most expensive vintage is predicted to be 1990, which is predicted to sell at 57.8 percent of the 1961 vintage price. (Remember that we are always dealing with prices relative to the 1961 price.) The next most expensive is 1989 at 53.6 percent, and then 1988 at 36.4 percent. The vintages 1987 and 1991 are not predicted to be very good, at 18.4 and 23.1 percent.

It is easy to see from Table 6-3 why the 1989 and 1990 vintages are predicted to be so good. The harvest season was very warm (18.60 and 18.70 degrees), and there was little rain in August and September (82 and 80 milliliters). On the other hand, the previous October–March period was not all that wet (443 and 468 milliliters), so the predicted price was high but not close to the 1961 price. You can also see why the 1987 vintage is not predicted to be very good: not a particularly warm harvest season, considerable rain in August and September, and not much rain the previous October–March.

To evaluate these predictions we need to decide what to compare the predictions to. The source of the vintage price data through 1980 was 1990–91 London auction prices, and 1990–91 is too soon for the 1987–91 vintages. (Remember that it takes a number of years before the true quality of a vintage is known.) To get some actual prices, on August 22, 2001, I called a local wine merchant in the New Haven area and inquired about wine prices for these vintages. These prices are in Table 6-5.

You can see that the prices range from $1,500 per bottle for a 1961 Latour to $30 for a 1987 Montrose. Aside from 1961, the most expensive wine is a 1990 Cheval Blanc at $500. Two averages are presented in Table 6-5. The first is the average across all six châteaux, and the second is the average across the last three. If there is a problem of conspicuous consumption or faddish buying, it seems more likely to show up in the prices for the very top châteaux than for the next group down. (Remember the last three châteaux are all *seconds crus*. Who can impress one's neighbors with merely a *second cru*?)

Now comes the punch line. We can compare the actual prices in Table 6-5 with the predicted prices in Table 6-4. The comparison is shown in Table 6-6. Table 6-6 requires a little explanation. The predicted values in Table 6-6 are from Table 6-4, and they are predicted prices relative to the 1961 price. The first column of actual values is based on the average of all six prices in Table 6-5. The 1987 value of .102, for example, is the ratio of 64.16 to 629.17. The 1988 value of .175 is the ratio of 110.00 to 629.17, and so on. The percentage errors using these actual values are presented in the next column. (Again, a percentage error is the logarithm of the predicted price minus the logarithm of the actual price.) The next column of actual values is based on the average of the last three châteaux's prices in Table 6-5. The 1987 value of .135 is the ratio of 35.00 to 258.33, the 1988 value of .271 is the ratio of 70.00 to 258.33, and so on. The percentage errors using these actual values are presented in the last column.

TABLE **6-5** Wine Prices per Bottle on August 22, 2001

	1961	1987	1988	1989	1990	1991
Latour	$1,500	$115	$140	$185	$400	$90
Lafite	700	80	165	190	225	75
Cheval Blanc	800	85	145	185	500	75
Pichon-Lalande	275	40	90	140	90	40
Cos d'Estournel	275	35	75	100	125	35
Montrose	225	30	45	95	225	35
Average (all 6)	629.17	64.16	110.00	149.17	260.83	58.33
Average (last 3)	258.33	35.00	70.00	111.67	146.67	36.67

Note: Prices obtained from Mt. Carmel Wine & Spirits, Hamden, Connecticut.

TABLE **6-6** Predicted Wine Prices by Vintage, 1987–1991

Vintage	Predicted Price	Actual Price (all 6)	Percentage Error	Actual Price (last 3)	Percentage Error
			(1961 = 1.000)		
1987	.184	.102	.590	.135	.310
1988	.364	.175	.732	.271	.295
1989	.536	.237	.816	.432	.216
1990	.578	.415	.331	.568	.017
1991	.231	.093	.910	.142	.487
Average			.676		.265

Table 6-6 contains a remarkable result. The average percentage error using the actual prices of the last three châteaux is .265, which is slightly smaller than the standard error of .286. Even though we are about a decade away from the end of the sample period, the predicted values are in line with what we would expect if the theory were accurate. The ranking of the five vintage years is the same for both the predicted values and actual values that are based on the last three châteaux: 1990, 1989, 1988, 1991, and 1987. If we stopped here, it would probably be cause for celebration—bring out a 1990 Pichon-Lalande!

Alas, there is a fly in the ointment. If we use all six châteaux's prices, the results are not nearly as good. You can see from the table that the average percentage error is .676, much higher than the standard error of .286. The predicted values are all much too high. The 1961 prices for the first three châteaux in Table 6-5 are very high relative to the prices for the other years, which means that all the ratios of the actual prices to the 1961 prices are very low. These ratios are not predicted to be this low, which leads to the large errors.

We are thus left with the conclusion that the theory does well if we take as actual prices the prices of the *seconds crus* châteaux, but not if we include the *premiers crus* châteaux (and Cheval Blanc). Remember that we are trying to explain wine quality, and we are using wine prices to measure wine quality. If wine prices deviate more from wine quality for the top châteaux than for the others (for conspicuous consumption or Robert Parker reasons), then this argues for using the *seconds crus* châteaux only, which is good for the theory.

There is another test of the theory that could be done. There are 36 bottles of wine represented in Table 6-5. We could take these bottles and do a blind taste test using, say, 20 wine experts (Robert Parker could be included). Each expert could rate each wine from, say, 1 to 10, and from these data we could create a quality index for each of the six vintages. The value of the index for a vintage would be its actual value, and the actual values could be compared to the predicted values as is done in Table 6-6. The theory could then be judged by how well the actual values were predicted. This comparison would have the advantage of eliminating any conspicuous consumption effects. (Another possibility to lessen the number of wines to be sampled would be to pour the six châteaux's wines for each vintage year into a large pitcher and to have the experts just sample each pitcher. I have been told that this is not a good idea.)

The taste test would also eliminate the problem of finding representative prices for the wines. If you, say, search for wine prices on the Internet, you will find that the same wine (same château and year) has a fairly wide range of prices. The wine prices in Table 6-5 have the advantage of all being chosen by the same store, but there is no guarantee that each price in the table is representative of prices of the wine elsewhere.

You might ask if this comparison using quality indices would be a good test of the theory since the theory was estimated using prices, not quality indices. The comparison would be a good test provided that the 1990–1991 prices, which were used in the estimation, were not influenced by conspicuous consumption effects and thus reflected the true quality of the wine. In other words, if the problem of prices not reflecting quality is a phenomenon that began after 1991, the coefficients in Box 6-2 are legitimate to use in a test using quality indices.

Can One Make Money?

Once the weather is known for a vintage (at the end of September of the vintage year), a prediction of the vintage price can be made using the coefficients in Box 6-2. This is an after-the-fact prediction since the actual values of the weather variables are used. It is also, however, a prediction that can't immediately be compared to the actual vintage price because the actual price is unknown. A number of years have to pass before the actual quality of the vintage is known and thus the actual price is known.

Since there are large auction markets for wine, including recently bottled wines, it is possible that one could make money buying or selling cases. If, for example, our prediction for the price of the current vintage is very high (because the three weather variables are favorable) and if the current auction price of the wine is much lower than this, one could make money by buying the wine now and selling it later (after the true quality of the wine becomes known and the price rises). If, on the other hand, our prediction is for a low price and the current auction price is higher, one should sell the wine short (if this is possible) and buy it back later. (If there are now conspicuous consumption effects for the top châteaux, it would be best to avoid these châteaux and concentrate on, say, the *seconds crus*.)

In other words, if you know something the auction market does not, you may be able to take advantage of it. In general, however, markets work fairly well, and it may be that the weather information has already been adequately incorporated into the current price. It may even be that some market participants are using the coefficients in Box 6-2 to make predictions! But then again, if most participants are like the editors of the *Wine Spectator,* there may be money to be made.

7 College Grades and Class Attendance

The student's life is pleasant,
 And pleasant is his labour,
Search all Ireland over
 You'll find no better neighbour.

Nor lords nor petty princes
 Dispute the student's pleasure,
Nor chapter stints his purse
 Nor stewardship his leisure.

None orders early rising,
 Calf-rearing or cow-tending,
Nor nights of toilsome vigil,
 His time is his for spending.

He takes a hand at draughts,
 And plucks a harp-string bravely,
And fills his nights with courting
 Some golden-haired light lady.

And when spring-time is come,
 The ploughshaft's there to follow,
A fistful of goosequills,
 And a straight deep furrow!

   Frank O'Connor, The Student

Much to the chagrin of both parents and teachers, many college students skip classes. Does skipping classes have any effect on a student's grade in a class? If it does, by how much? We will see in this chapter that grades do suffer if more than four classes are skipped in a semester, so there is some cost to students who skip many classes. I begin my courses by pointing out this result in the hope that students will see the light and think twice about any planned skipping behavior.

Although the focus of this chapter is on class attendance, the results are of more general interest. The basic question is what determines a student's grade in a class, and we will see that there are many variables that matter. This chapter is based on an article by Garey C. Durden and Larry V. Ellis, "The Effects of Attendance on Student Learning in Principles of Economics," *American Economic Review* (May 1995), 343–46.

Theory and Data

The variable to be explained is a student's grade in a principles of economics course in a medium-sized college in North Carolina. The grade is in percentage terms, ranging from 0 to 100 percent. Students were sampled over three semesters—spring and fall 1993 and spring 1994. The number of students sampled was 346. The data from these surveys are listed in Table 7-1.

The first variable in Table 7-1 is the dependent variable—grade. As just noted, it is in percentage terms. This is the grade in the principles of economics course.

A typical procedure in a study like this is to include as many explanatory variables in the analysis as seem theoretically plausible. Theory is used to exclude unlikely variables, so the variables that remain have a ring of plausibility to them. Then the best fitting set of coefficients is found using all the theoretically plausible variables and the *t*-statistics are computed and examined. Explanatory variables with *t*-statistics greater than about 2.0 or less than about −2.0 are taken to be significant, and the rest are not. Variables that are not significant are usually dropped from the analysis. The variables in Table 7-1 are meant to be plausible theoretical candidates for explaining the course grade. We will see in the next section how many are significant.

Let's go through the variables in Table 7-1 one by one. There are five variables that measure absences from class: skip12, skip34, skip56, skip78, and skip 9+. For example, skip12 has a value of 1 if the student has skipped only 1 or 2 classes and a value of 0 otherwise. Using these five variables allows us to see how many classes can be skipped (if any) without having the course grade suffer.

TABLE **7-1** Data for Testing the Theory That Class Attendance Affects Grades

Variable	Description	Mean
grade	Student course grade (%)	72.234
skip12	1 if 1 or 2 absences; 0 otherwise	.277
skip34	1 if 3 or 4 absences; 0 otherwise	.159
skip56	1 if 5 or 6 absences; 0 otherwise	.162
skip78	1 if 7 or 8 absences; 0 otherwise	.061
skip9+	1 if 9 or more absences; 0 otherwise	.104
SATmath	Math SAT score	515.647
SATverbal	Verbal SAT score	466.960
GPA	Grade point average (4-point scale times 100)	269.538
colprep	1 if high school program was college prep; 0 otherwise	.538
HSecon	1 if had high school economics; 0 otherwise	.454
calculus	1 if have taken college calculus; 0 otherwise	.532
econ	1 if previously had a college economics course; 0 otherwise	.419
hoursstudy	Number of hours per week studying economics	2.400
hourswork	Number of hours worked per week in a job	7.818
credithours	Number of credit hours carried during current semester	13.081
extracurr	1 if one or more extracurricular activities; 0 otherwise	.720
fratsor	1 if fraternity or sorority member; 0 otherwise	.214
parents	0 if either of the student's parents had a high school education or less; 1 if either parent had some college; 2 if either parent had a college degree; and 3 if either parent studied at the graduate level	1.621
white	1 if white; 0 otherwise	.951
male	1 if male; 0 if female	.621
local	1 if from North Carolina; 0 otherwise	.899

SATmath is the student's SAT math score, and SATverbal is the student's SAT verbal score. To the extent that SAT scores measure academic ability, they should have a positive effect on the course grade; high ability students should do better, other things being equal, than low ability ones. A measure of both ability and motivation is the student's overall grade point average (GPA) before enrolling in the course. We would expect the variable GPA to have a positive effect on the course grade.

The next four variables pertain to the student's high school and college preparation. The variable colprep is 1 if the student's high school program was college prep and is 0 otherwise. The variable HSecon is 1 if the student has had high school economics and is 0 otherwise. The variable calculus is 1 if the student has had college calculus and is 0 otherwise. The variable econ is 1 if the student has previously had a college economics course and is 0 otherwise. We would expect these four variables to have a positive effect on the course grade.

The next five variables concern how the student spends his or her time in college. The variable hoursstudy is the number of hours per week spent studying economics, hourswork is the number of hours worked per week in a job, and credithours is the number of credit hours carried during the current semester. The variable extracurr is 1 if the student has one or more extracurricular activities and is 0 otherwise, and fratsor is 1 if the student belongs to a fraternity or sorority and is 0 otherwise. We would expect hoursstudy to have a positive effect on the course grade and the other four to have a negative effect.

The variable parents is meant to pick up family background effects. It is a measure of the amount of schooling the student's parents have had. The variable male is 1 if the student is male and 0 if female. The variable white is 1 if the student is white and is 0 otherwise. Finally, the variable local is 1 if the student is from North Carolina (the home state) and is 0 if not.

To summarize, the 21 variables in Table 7-1 after grade, which is the dependent variable, are possible variables that affect the student's course grade. The theory is that these variables may matter in terms of affecting how well the student does in the course. We will see in the next section which ones seem to matter and which do not.

Fit, Test, and Examine the Results

There are 22 coefficients to estimate: the coefficient for each of the explanatory variables in Table 7-1 plus the intercept. The best fitting set of coefficients was found in the usual way, and the t-statistics were computed. The results are shown in Box 7-1.

Let's get right to the main point. Does class attendance matter? You can see that skip12 and skip34 are not significant, but that skip56 and skip 9+ are, and skip78 nearly is (t-statistic of -1.83). The results thus say that if you skip five or more classes, your grade will suffer. For example, the coefficient for skip56 is -3.228, which says that with five or six absences the grade falls 3.228 percentage points. So it does not matter for the first four absences (because skip12 and skip34 have small

BOX **7-1**

grade depends on:		t-statistic
0.465	skip12	0.38
−1.538	skip34	−1.11
−3.228	skip56	−2.29
−3.475	skip78	−1.83
−3.521	skip9+	2.12
0.011	SATmath	1.97
0.014	SATverbal	2.35
0.078	GPA	9.13
−0.097	colprep	0.11
2.766	HSecon	3.35
3.352	calculus	3.75
−1.027	econ	1.19
0.093	hoursstudy	0.41
−0.049	hourswork	1.28
−0.021	credithours	0.27
−0.595	extracurr	0.60
−1.886	fratsor	1.80
0.695	parents	1.83
4.524	white	2.33
0.736	male	0.80
−0.737	local	−0.54
33.919	intercept	3.94
number of observations: 346		

t-statistics and are thus not significant), but after that it does. This result, of course, seems sensible. Missing a few classes is probably not a big deal, but there is a limit.

What about the other variables? The three variables measuring ability matter. SATmath has a t-statistic of 1.97, which is essentially 2.0, and SATverbal has a t-statistic of 2.35. The variable GPA has a huge *t*-statistic (9.13) and is thus highly significant. Not surprisingly, how a student has done in previous courses is significant in explaining how the student will do in the principles of economics course.

The HSecon variable is significant (*t*-statistic of 3.35), and the calculus variable is significant (*t*-statistic of 3.75). It thus matters whether the student has had economics in high school and whether he or she has had calculus. The estimated effects are fairly large. The coefficient for calculus is 3.352, so calculus adds 3.352 percentage points to the course grade, other things being equal. The coefficient for HSecon is 2.766.

There is only one other variable in Box 7-1 that is significant, which is the variable white. The coefficient is 4.524 and the *t*-statistic is 2.33. This says that, other things being equal, white students score 4.524 percentage points higher than nonwhite students. It is unclear what is going on here. Only 4.9 percent of the students in the sample are nonwhite, and this result may be a fluke in the sense that the large coefficient is heavily influenced by a few very low nonwhite scores. If the result is not a fluke, it says there is something in the background of nonwhite students not captured by the other explanatory variables that has a negative effect on the course grade.

Two other variables are close to being significant: parents, with a *t*-statistic of 1.83, and fratsor, with a *t*-statistic of –1.80. Both may thus play a role. The coefficient for fratsor is –1.89, which means that being a Greek, other things being equal, lowers your score by 1.89 percentage points.

All the remaining variables have *t*-statistics that lead to their rejection as explanatory variables. These are colprep, hoursstudy, hourswork, credithours, extracurr, male, and local. Since these variables are rejected, one could reestimate the coefficients with these variables excluded. Box 7-1 would then have seven fewer coefficients. The authors of the study did not do this in their article, so I cannot present it here.

If these results are to be trusted (we will discuss possible pitfalls in the next section), they may be of use to college administrators. One possibility, for example, would be to require calculus, since calculus is quite significant. Another possibility would be to take attendance to discourage students from skipping more than about four classes. For large lecture courses, I have suggested putting chips in shoes, as is done in road races, where the chips would be recorded as the students enter the lecture hall. This suggestion has not been received with open arms, but the technology is still new to some people.

Possible Pitfalls

The above results are based on a survey of students in one type of course (principles of economics) in one type of college (middle-sized, in North Carolina). It may be that the effects are different in different courses and colleges, so generalizing these results to other courses and colleges is somewhat risky. In particular, some of the rejected variables could be significant in other studies.

It is important to realize what we mean by the effects possibly being different in other courses and colleges. We know from Chapter 5 that a sample need not be a random draw from a population in order for the results to be valid. In the case of the extramarital affairs data, the sample does not have to be a random draw from the population as long as the selection criterion does not depend on the size of the dependent variable (that is, selection bias does not exist). When we say this, however, we are assuming that the coefficients are the same for everyone. As we discussed in Chapter 5, people can differ in the values of the explanatory variables, but not in the coefficients that are attached to these variables. If coefficients differ across groups of individuals, we must treat each group separately in the sense of finding the best fitting set of coefficients group by group.

For the present example we are thus saying that the coefficients that pertain to students in the principles of economics course in a middle-sized college in North Carolina may not be the same as the coefficients in other courses and colleges. If this is so, then the results in Box 7-1 cannot be generalized.

Another possible pitfall is that some students may have filled out the survey incorrectly. If there are errors in measuring the explanatory variables, the coefficient estimates for these variables will in general be incorrect (biased). For example, it is a little odd that the hoursstudy variable is not significant, as shown in Box 7-1, and it could be that students did not do a good job of estimating their study hours in the survey.

Predict

If we exclude the insignificant variables in Box 7-1, we know at the beginning of the semester everything we need to know about the student except the skip variables. By making assumptions about the skip variables for a given student, we can thus predict his or her course grade. Say that, under the assumption that the student skips no classes, the predicted course grade is 81.000 percent, a B−. Now say the student is planning to skip five classes. The predicted value is now 81.000 minus 3.228 (the coefficient estimate for skip56), which is 77.772, a C+. We would thus advise the student that skipping the five classes could lower his or her grade from a B− to a C+.

As a final word of warning, remember that there are errors attached to any prediction. We have not discussed the size of the standard error in this chapter. The article upon which this chapter is based did not in fact present the standard error. Its main concern was whether the skip variables were significant and what the sizes of their coefficients were. There is, however, undoubtedly a nontrivial standard error, so any prediction has uncertainty attached to it.

8   Marathon Times

If you can fill the unforgiving minute
  With sixty seconds' worth of distance run,
Yours is the Earth and everything that's in it,
  And—which is more—you'll be a Man, my son!
    Rudyard Kipling, from If—

Do not go gentle into that good night,
Old age should burn and rave at close of day;
Rage, rage against the dying of the light.
    Dylan Thomas, from Do Not Go Gentle into That Good Night

This chapter, my favorite, is concerned with a particular physical activity, namely, running marathons. Although most readers of this book probably have never run a marathon (if they have, I am probably not selling many books), it is never too late to start. Marathon running is life writ small. With its work, strategy, pain and pleasure of pushing oneself to the limits, disappointment at doing poorly, joy of doing well, and, alas, the inevitable slowing down with age, it mimics much of what life is about.

The question considered in this chapter is how marathon times change with age. If you ran a marathon in three hours at age 35, what can you expect to do at age 50 or at age 70? We want to estimate the rate at which people slow down with age.

Although the focus in this chapter is on marathon times, the analysis has broader implications. The broader question concerns the rate at which people physically deteriorate with age. How much, for example, can be physically expected of a healthy, non-injured 75-year-old man or woman relative to what he or she could do at age 45? If we can get good estimates of how fast people physically deteriorate, we can use these estimates to think about social policies on aging. Policies on aging should obviously depend on the rate at which deterioration occurs. If, for example, the rate remains small into fairly old age, then policies designed to keep people physically fit will have more payoff than if the rate increases rapidly with age. The size of the rate is also relevant for retirement policies. The smaller the rate, the less emphasis should probably be placed on plans to encourage people to retire earlier than they would otherwise want to. The size of the rate may also be relevant for the question of how wage rates should change with age.

A Theory of the Slowdown Rate

It is obvious that people slow down with age. No one expects a world-class 60-year-old marathoner to be competitive with a world-class 30-year-old marathoner. However, we would like to know more than this. We would like to know what the slowdown rate is at different ages. What is the slowdown rate at age 50, at age 60, at age 70, and so on? The theory that we are going to use is depicted in Figure 8-1. The time taken

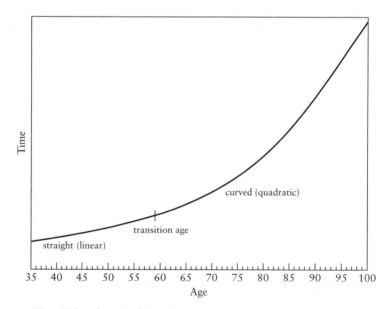

FIGURE **8-1** Time Taken for a Task by Age

for a task is represented on the vertical axis, and age is on the horizontal axis. The vertical axis is measured in percentage terms, which means that equal distances on the vertical axis mean equal percentage changes. For example, the distance on the vertical axis from 10 to 15, an increase of 50 percent, is the same as the distance on the vertical axis from 100 to 150, also an increase of 50 percent. We are using the percentage scale because we want to base the theory in percentage terms. *Slowdown rate* in this chapter means percentage slowdown.

The line in Figure 8-1 shows that between age 35 and some transition age, the percentage increase in the time taken for a task is the same from year to year. For example, if at age 41 the slowdown rate is 1.0 percent, it is also 1.0 percent at age 42. Until the transition age, we slow down each year, but the *size* of the slowdown rate does not change.

At the transition age the line begins to curve upward, which means that the slowdown rate begins to increase. For example, if at age 70 the slowdown rate were 1.8 percent, at age 71 it would be larger, say 1.9 percent. The curve reflects the idea that at some age things begin to get worse faster. The curve in Figure 8-1 is a *quadratic*. The quadratic curve has the feature that the *increase* in the slowdown rate is the same from age to age. For example, if from age 71 to 72 the slowdown rate increases from 1.9 percent to 2.0 percent, then from age 72 to 73 it will increase from 2.0 percent to 2.1 percent. The 0.1 increase is the same from age to age.

The main idea behind Figure 8-1 is simple, even trivial. It is that at least by age 35 people begin to slow down and that at some age the slowdown rate begins to increase. The two specific assumptions represented in the figure are (1) the slowdown rate does not change between age 35 and some transition age and (2) the increase in the slowdown rate after the transition rate is the same from age to age.

While the main idea behind Figure 8-1 is obvious, what is not so obvious is how we determine the line. The three things we need to determine it are (1) the slowdown rate before the transition age, (2) the transition age, and (3) the amount by which the slowdown rate increases from year to year after the transition age. The data that are used for this purpose are discussed next.

The Data

What data might we use to determine the line in Figure 8-1? Since we are focusing on the marathon, one possibility is to take an individual who has run a marathon every year and use his or her times to fit the line. The problem with this is that any one runner has good years and bad years, depending on motivation, injury, weather during the race, and so forth, so we may not be sampling a person's best effort each year.

Another possibility is to consider each point on the line in Figure 8-1 to be the biological minimum for that age across all humans, the fastest time that the best human of that age could run. We have, fortunately, an observation of this time, which is the world record for that age. World records for the marathon by age are presented in Table 8-1. The

TABLE **8-1** Best Marathon Times by Age

Age	Time	Record Holder	Race	Race Date
35	2:12:13	Paul Pilkington	City of Los Angeles	3/6/94
37	2:12:51	Steve Plasencia	Twin Cities	10/2/94
39	2:14:20	Steve Plasencia	Olympic Trials: Charlotte	2/17/96
40	2:17:02	Kenneth Judson	Rocket City	12/8/90
41	2:19:21	Doug Kurtis	Revco-Cleveland	5/16/93
42	2:20:00	Doug Kurtis	Twin Cities	10/2/94
43	2:22:48	Jim Bowers	Humboldt Redwoods	10/10/82
44	2:22:55	Doug Kurtis	WZYP Rocket City	12/14/90
45	2:25:50	Jim Bowers	Humboldt Redwoods	10/14/84
52	2:25:51	Norm Green	Wigal Champ	12/2/84
53	2:31:20	Norm Green	Marine Corps	11/3/85
54	2:32:28	Norm Green	Lincoln	5/3/87
55	2:33:49	Norm Green	Lincoln	5/1/88
58	2:37:40	Alex Ratelle	Nike OTC	9/12/82
58	2:37:40	Norm Green	Twin Cities	10/14/90
64	2:42:44	Clive Davies	Portland	10/28/79
66	2:42:48	Clive Davies	Nike OTC	9/13/81
68	2:52:45	Clive Davies	Lincoln	5/6/84
69	3:00:57	Monty Montgomery	Western Hemisphere	12/7/75
71	3:00:58	John Keston	Twin Cities	10/6/96
72	3:09:10	Warren Utes	Twin Cities	10/4/92
73	3:12:44	Warren Utes	Twin Cities	10/3/93
75	3:18:10	Warren Utes	LaSalle Banks Chicago	10/15/95
77	3:33:27	Ed Benham	Wigal Champ	12/2/84
78	3:36:59	Warren Utes	Twin Cities	10/4/98
79	3:49:23	Ed Benham	Calloway Gardens	1/10/87
84	4:17:51	Ed Benham	Twin Cities	10/6/91

times increase from 2:12:13 (2 hours, 12 minutes, 13 seconds) for age 35 to 4:17:51 for age 84. We will use the data in Table 8-1 to determine the line in Figure 8-1. The line will allow us to determine the slowdown rate, the transition age, and the increase in the slowdown rate after the transition age.

Before we fit the data, however, we need to pause to consider whether what we are doing is sensible. Where might we go wrong? The most serious problem is that some of the times may not be close to the biological minimum. Since hundreds of thousands of people age 35 have run a marathon, the world record for that age is probably close to the best time that could ever be run—the biological minimum. On the other hand, far fewer people age 84 have run a marathon, so the current world record for that age may not be that close to the best that could ever be done. Think about it this way. If in the next 20 years hundreds of thousands of people age 84 run a marathon, the time of 4:17:51 in Table 8-1 might be lowered considerably. On the other hand, if in the next 20 years hundreds of thousands of people age 35 run a marathon, the currently best time of 2:12:13 may be lowered only slightly. In other words, at older ages we may currently have a *small sample problem*.

Two procedures were followed in an attempt to mitigate the effects of the small sample problem. The first is not to use any times after age 84. There are marathon records through age 92, but there are so few people age 92 who have run a marathon that the record seems unlikely to be near the biological minimum. In case you are curious, the world record for age 92 is 9:23:25, set by Paul Spangler in the New York City Marathon in 1991. The world record for age 90 is 7:52:16, set by James Ramsey in the Detroit Free Press Marathon in 1998. These times are not included in Table 8-1 because they were not used.

The second procedure was to exclude any age for which the time was slower than a time for an older age. For example, there is no age 46 in Table 8-1 because the time for this age, 2:26:21, is slower than the age 52 time of 2:25:51. Since we don't expect times to decrease with age, any age for which the time is slower than the time for an older age must suffer from the small sample problem. Since we know that the biological minimum for age 52 is at least 2:25:51, the biological minimum for age 46 must be lower than this. We would expect the age 46 time to come down substantially in the future as we get a larger sample of 46-year-olds running marathons.

A good example of the use of the second procedure concerns Norm Green, who you can see from the table holds the record for ages 52, 53, 54, 55, and 58. Green also holds the record for age 51, but his time at age 51 was 2:29:11, which is slower than his time at age 52 of 2:25:51. Green's age 51 time is not included in the table. As good as his time was at age 51, it was obviously not his biological minimum. Green ran his first marathon at age 49, so he may have still been learning at age 51.

You might ask, what if all ages are getting faster over time because of things like better nutrition, better training methods, better shoes, and so on? Fortunately, this problem is not serious as long as all ages are getting better at the same rate. All this would do is shift the line down in Figure 8-1. It would not affect the slowdown rate, the transition age, or the increase in the slowdown rate after the transition age. Progress would be a problem only if it differently affected the various ages.

Because progress may be made in the future at all ages, our use of the term *biological minimum* is not quite right. To be precise, we should put *almost* in front of it.

Fit

Now comes the fun part, which is to find the line that best fits the times in Table 8-1. The line in Figure 8-1 is determined by four coefficients: the intercept, the slope up to the transition age, the transition age, and the increase in the slope after the transition age. You may think about a computer trying thousands of lines like that in the figure (that is, thousands of sets of four coefficients) and choosing the line that provides the smallest sum of squared errors. This would be the best fitting line.

In the present case, however, there is a restriction we want to impose. We would like none of the times to be below the line. If the line is to reflect the biological minimum at each age, it would not make sense to have any time be below the minimum. This restriction is imposed by simply having the computer try only lines that lie below all the times. The error for each age is the distance from the time to the line. The computer calculates all the errors, squares them, and then adds them up. Each line thus has a sum of squared errors associated with it, and the computer finds the one with the smallest sum.

For computational reasons, we did not in fact require that absolutely all times lie above the line, and in fact four of the times were slightly below the line. As we discussed before, a point on the line is not meant to be the exact biological minimum, just almost that.

The line that gives the best fit subject to the restriction that almost all the times lie above the line is shown in Figure 8-2. You can see that the transition age is 59.6 years. Before this age the slowdown rate is constant—0.62 percent per year. After age 59.6 the slowdown rate increases each year, and the amount of the increase is 0.12 percent per year. Three of the four coefficients are thus 59.6 for the transition age, 0.62 for the slowdown rate before the transition age, and 0.12 for the increase in the slowdown rate after the transition age. The fourth coefficient, the intercept, determines the vertical position of the line in Figure 8-2. The line crosses the age 35 axis at a time of 2:11:24.

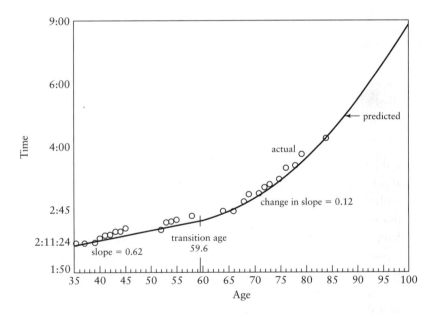

FIGURE **8-2** Actual and Predicted Best Marathon Times by Age

We are not looking at *t*-statistics, because their use in this case is not the best way to test the theory. It is obvious that none of the coefficients are zero. For example, no one would think that the slowdown rate is zero or that after some age the slowdown rate does not begin to increase. The procedure to be used here is to fit the line and then examine what the fitted line implies.

Table 8-2 presents some useful information about the line. This table is the same as Table 8-1 except that the points on the line are presented along with the deviations of the actual times from the line. The point on the line for a given age will be called the *potential* time. Keep in mind, however, that *potential* is not exactly the same as *biological limit*, because the computer was not forced to have all times above the line. The deviation from a time to the line is the difference between the actual time and the potential time. This deviation for a given age is the error for that age.

You can see from Table 8-2 that for a number of ages the actual time is considerably larger than the potential time. For age 45, for example, the actual time (by Jim Bowers) is 2:25:50, and the potential time is 2:20:00, for a difference of 5 minutes and 50 seconds. The actual time for age 52, on the other hand, is essentially on the line. The actual time (by Norm Green) is 2:25:51, and the potential time is 30 seconds more at 2:26:21. If the line is accurate, in the future we should expect to see the age 45 time falling by about 6 minutes and the age 52 time falling little if any.

The times for other ages that should fall by 5 minutes or more if the line is accurate are those for ages 58, 69, 72, 73, 77, and 79. The difference for age 79, for example, is 9 minutes and 52 seconds. On the other hand, the difference for age 84 is essentially zero. For both ages 79 and 84 Ed Benham holds the record, so the line tells us that Benham's performance at age 84 is much closer to the biological limit than is his performance at age 79 (way to go, Ed!). We should thus expect runners to have a better shot at the age 79 record, where the record could be lowered by nearly 10 minutes, than at the age 84 record.

The actual times in Table 8-2 were used to determine the line in Figure 8-2. Remember that not all ages' times were used. Dominated times (times that are larger than a time for an older age) were not used, and times above age 84 were not used. However, once the line is chosen,

TABLE **8-2** Actual and Potential Best Marathon Times by Age

Age	Actual Time	Potential Time	Actual Minus Potential	Record Holder	Race	Race Date
35	2:12:13	2:11:24	0:49	Paul Pilkington	City of Los Angeles	3/6/94
37	2:12:51	2:13:04	−0:13	Steve Plasencia	Twin Cities	10/2/94
39	2:14:20	2:14:46	−0:26	Steve Plasencia	Olympic Trials: Charlotte	2/17/96
40	2:17:02	2:15:38	1:24	Kenneth Judson	Rocket City	12/8/90
41	2:19:21	2:16:29	2:52	Doug Kurtis	Revco-Cleveland	5/16/93
42	2:20:00	2:17:21	2:39	Doug Kurtis	Twin Cities	10/2/94
43	2:22:48	2:18:14	4:34	Jim Bowers	Humboldt Redwoods	10/10/82
44	2:22:55	2:19:07	3:48	Doug Kurtis	WZYP Rocket City	12/14/96
45	2:25:50	2:20:00	5:50	Jim Bowers	Humboldt Redwoods	10/14/84
52	2:25:51	2:26:21	−0:30	Norm Green	Wigal Champ	12/2/84
53	2:31:20	2:27:17	4:03	Norm Green	Marine Corps	11/3/85
54	2:32:28	2:28:13	4:15	Norm Green	Lincoln	5/3/87
55	2:33:49	2:29:10	4:39	Norm Green	Lincoln	5/1/88
58	2:37:40	2:32:02	5:38	Alex Ratelle	Nike OTC	9/12/82
58	2:37:40	2:32:02	5:38	Norm Green	Twin Cities	10/14/90
64	2:42:44	2:40:14	2:30	Clive Davies	Portland	10/28/79
66	2:42:48	2:44:34	−1:46	Clive Davies	Nike OTC	9/13/81
68	2:52:45	2:49:49	2:56	Clive Davies	Lincoln	5/6/84
69	3:00:57	2:52:49	8:08	Monty Montgomery	Western Hemisphere	12/7/75
71	3:00:58	2:59:35	1:23	John Keston	Twin Cities	10/6/96
72	3:09:10	3:03:24	5:46	Warren Utes	Twin Cities	10/4/92
73	3:12:44	3:07:30	5:14	Warren Utes	Twin Cities	10/3/93
75	3:18:10	3:16:42	1:28	Warren Utes	LaSalle Banks Chicago	10/15/95
77	3:33:27	3:27:18	6:09	Ed Benham	Wigal Champ	12/2/84
78	3:36:59	3:33:12	3:47	Warren Utes	Twin Cities	10/4/98
79	3:49:23	3:39:31	9:52	Ed Benham	Calloway Gardens	1/10/87
84	4:17:51	4:18:33	−0:42	Ed Benham	Twin Cities	10/6/91

it can be used to predict times for all ages above 35, not just the ages in Table 8-2. The *potential* (predicted) time for a given age is simply the point on the line for that age. Table 8-3 presents the actual and potential times for these other ages. As expected, the potential time for each of these ages is less than the actual time, in many cases by a large amount. For example, the age 50 potential time is 9 minutes and 51 seconds below the actual time, and the age 60 potential time is 13 minutes and 43 seconds below the actual time.

TABLE **8-3** Actual and Potential Best Marathon Times by Age: Dominated Times

Age	Actual Time	Potential Time	Actual Minus Potential	Record Holder	Race	Race Date
36	2:15:35	2:12:14	3:21	Don Janicki	Revco-Cleveland	5/5/96
38	2:17:26	2:13:55	3:31	Budd Coates	Olympic Trials: Charlotte	2/17/96
46	2:26:21	2:20:53	5:28	Jim Bowers	Humboldt Redwoods	10/13/85
47	2:26:43	2:21:47	4:56	Bob Schlau	Houston-Tenneco	1/15/95
48	2:30:45	2:22:41	8:04	Jim Knerr	Santa Monica	8/29/82
49	2:33:03	2:23:36	9:27	Ken Sparks	Detroit Free Press	10/16/94
50	2:34:21	2:24:30	9:51	Michael Heffernan	Twin Cities	10/14/90
51	2:29:11	2:25:26	3:45	Norm Green	Lincoln	5/6/84
56	2:38:55	2:30:07	8:48	Alex Ratelle	City of Lakes	10/19/80
57	2:38:07	2:31:04	7:03	Alex Ratelle	Madeline Island	9/12/81
59	2:48:25	2:33:00	15:25	Alex Ratelle	Omaha Waterfront	11/5/83
60	2:47:46	2:34:03	13:43	Clive Davies	Nike OTC	10/12/75
61	2:43:11	2:35:18	7:53	Gaylon Jorgensen	Twin Cities	10/14/90
62	2:49:06	2:36:45	12:21	Norm Green	Twin Cities	10/2/94
63	2:48:04	2:38:23	9:41	Clive Davies	Track Capital	5/6/79
65	2:51:27	2:42:17	9:10	Clive Davies	Trails End	2/28/81
67	2:55:15	2:47:05	8:10	Clive Davies	Emerald City	3/27/83
70	3:01:14	2:56:04	5:10	Warren Utes	Old Style Chicago	10/28/90
74	3:37:07	3:11:56	25:11	Ed Benham	Marine Corps	11/1/81
76	3:34:42	3:21:49	12:53	Ed Benham	Marine Corps	11/6/83
80	4:28:01	3:46:17	41:44	Bill Brobston	Twin Cities	10/3/93
81	4:50:00	3:53:33	56:27	Paul Spangler	Avenue of Giants	5/4/80
82	4:38:00	4:01:19	36:41	Dudley Healy	Twin Cities	10/6/96
83	5:20:08	4:09:38	1:10:30	Max Bayne	British American	12/16/84
85	5:21:51	4:28:06	53:45	Paul Spangler	Wigal Champ	12/2/84
86	5:40:10	4:38:19	1:01:51	Ivor Welch	Avenue of Giants	5/3/81
87	6:48:44	4:49:17	1:59:27	Ivor Welch	San Francisco	7/11/82
88	6:52:30	5:01:01	1:51:29	Abraham Weintraub	Flura London,GBR	4/26/98
89	6:35:38	5:13:36	1:22:02	Sam Gadless	City of Los Angeles	3/3/96
90	7:52:16	5:27:06	2:25:10	James Ramsey	Detroit Free Press	10/18/98
91	none	5:41:34				
92	9:23:25	5:57:06	3:26:19	Paul Spangler	New York City	11/3/91
93	none	6:13:47				
94	none	6:31:42				
95	none	6:50:57				
96	none	7:11:40				
97	none	7:33:58				
98	none	7:57:58				
99	none	8:23:49				
100	none	8:51:42				

Note: If a best time for an age is larger than the best time for an older age, it is a *dominated time*.

Before discussing Table 8-3 further, let's pause for a moment and think about testing. What evidence would call into question the aging theory that is represented graphically in Figure 8-1? The most damaging evidence would be times for the older ages that are considerably below the line. This evidence would suggest that the line has overestimated the speed with which people physically deteriorate with age. If this happened, a different shape of the line would have to be postulated and new estimates made. If, on the other hand, only a few times turn out to fall below the line and the amounts they fall below are small, this would provide support for the theory. To test our theory we thus have to wait for a larger sample of marathon times.

Fortunately, as previously discussed, the theory is not affected if all ages are getting better over time because of things like better nutrition and better training methods. This would mean that after a while all times would lie below the line in Figure 8-2, but if they were all roughly the same distance below the line, they would not affect in any serious way the slowdown rate, the transition age, and the increase in the slowdown rate. They would just affect the intercept.

The theory is probably the most vulnerable for the oldest ages. For example, it may not be sensible to assume that the increase in the slowdown rate remains constant after age 85 or so. Maybe there should be a second transition age after which the slowdown rate increases by a larger amount each year. In other words, the quadratic curve might be a good approximation between about ages 60 and 85, and after 85 a steeper curve might be needed. We don't yet have enough observations at the oldest ages to be able to say much.

Table 8-3 shows the implications of the present theory (that is, the use of the quadratic curve from the transition age on up) for the oldest ages. Remember from Table 8-2 that Ed Benham ran a time of 4:17:51 at age 84. Following the line up in age, the table shows a potential time at age 89 of 5:13:36. In other words, a runner is predicted to lose about 56 minutes in five years. The current record (by Sam Gadless) for age 89 is 6:35:38, which is about 1 hour and 22 minutes slower than the potential time. Is the line's prediction too optimistic here, or can we expect in the future someone age 89 to run a 5:13:36 marathon? Again, we don't really know. We need a much larger sample of 89-year-olds finishing a marathon.

If we take the line all the way to age 100, we get a potential time of 8:51:42. There are no records beyond age 92, so we have no idea whether this is feasible or not. An 8:51:42 marathon is about 20 minutes a mile, so all we need is a 100-year-old puttering along at about 3 miles an hour. The problem may not be the first few miles, but all 26.2 of them.

Use the Results

If we are willing to take the line in Figure 8-2 as being a good approximation, at least up to about age 85, we can do some useful things with it. We can first compute what are called *age-graded factors* or *age factors*. These are presented in Table 8-4. We let the age factor for age 35 be 1.0, and we then increase it by the estimated slowdown rates. For example, the slowdown rate for age 36 is 0.62 percent, so the age factor for age 36 is 0.62 percent larger than 1.0, or 1.0062 (rounded to 1.006 in the table). The percentage changes in the factors in Table 8-4 are simply the slowdown rates. For one more example, the age factor for age 70 is 1.338 and the slowdown rate for age 71 is 2.04 percent. Therefore, the age factor for age 71 is 2.04 percent greater than 1.338, or 1.365.

People may differ in how they read Table 8-4, but I am struck by how small the deterioration rates are. The age factor for age 75, for example, is 1.499, only 32 percent larger than the age factor of 1.133 for age 55. The deterioration rate is thus only 32 percent over these 20 years. Even someone age 85 is only about twice as slow as he was at age 35. Given these numbers, societies may have been too pessimistic about losses from aging for individuals who stay healthy and fit. Societies may have passed laws dealing with older people under incorrect assumptions.

If we leave society for now and turn to individuals, does Table 8-4 have anything to say about you and me? Remember that the age factors in the table are based on results using data from world-class athletes. Since most of us are not world-class athletes, what can we learn? Fortunately, one assumption is all you and I need to be able to use the table on a personal basis. This assumption is that we differ from a world-class athlete by a certain percent and this percent does not change as we age. If at age 35 when in peak condition I am slower than a world-class athlete of the same age by 50 percent, then the assumption is that at age 70 in peak condition I am also slower than a world-class athlete of the same

TABLE **8-4** Age-Graded Factors for the Marathon

Age	Age-Graded Factor	Percentage Change in Factor	Age	Age-Graded Factor	Percentage Change in Factor
35	1.000	0.62	68	1.290	1.67
36	1.006	0.62	69	1.313	1.80
37	1.013	0.62	70	1.338	1.92
38	1.019	0.62	71	1.365	2.04
39	1.025	0.62	72	1.395	2.17
40	1.032	0.62	73	1.427	2.29
41	1.038	0.62	74	1.462	2.42
42	1.045	0.62	75	1.499	2.54
43	1.051	0.62	76	1.538	2.66
44	1.058	0.62	77	1.581	2.79
45	1.064	0.62	78	1.628	2.91
46	1.071	0.62	79	1.677	3.04
47	1.078	0.62	80	1.730	3.16
48	1.084	0.62	81	1.787	3.28
49	1.091	0.62	82	1.848	3.41
50	1.098	0.62	83	1.913	3.53
51	1.105	0.62	84	1.983	3.66
52	1.112	0.62	85	2.058	3.78
53	1.119	0.62	86	2.138	3.91
54	1.126	0.62	87	2.224	4.03
55	1.133	0.62	88	2.316	4.15
56	1.140	0.62	89	2.416	4.28
57	1.147	0.62	90	2.522	4.40
58	1.154	0.62	91	2.636	4.53
59	1.161	0.62	92	2.759	4.65
60	1.169	0.68	93	2.890	4.77
61	1.178	0.80	94	3.032	4.90
62	1.189	0.93	95	3.184	5.02
63	1.202	1.05	96	3.348	5.15
64	1.216	1.17	97	3.524	5.27
65	1.232	1.30	98	3.714	5.39
66	1.249	1.42	99	3.919	5.52
67	1.269	1.55	100	4.141	5.64

age by 50 percent. In other words, my slowdown rate is assumed to be the same as that of world-class athletes; I am just starting from a higher base (that is, a slower time).

Given this assumption, people over age 35 can use Table 8-4 on a personal basis. For example, my best marathon performance (so far) has been a time of 2:58:45 in 1987 at the Philadelphia Marathon. I was 45 at the time. In 1989, then 47, I ran 3:01:45 at the New York City

Marathon. The age factor for age 45 in the table is 1.064, and the age factor for age 47 is 1.078, an increase of 1.32 percent. My New York City time is 1.68 percent higher than my Philadelphia time, so I was fairly close to staying on the line (that is, on my personal potential line).

Alas, I am currently struggling to get back on the line. In 2001 at age 59 I ran the Mystic Places Marathon in 3:30:23. How good is this time? We can use the age factors in Table 8-4 to see that this time is not very good. The table shows that between ages 45 and 59 the age factor goes from 1.064 to 1.161, an increase of 9.1 percent. Given my time of 2:58:45 at age 45, the estimated age factors thus suggest that at age 59 I should have been able to run 3:15:03, which is 9.1 percent greater than my age 45 time. I thus ran about 15 minutes slower than I should have been able to do. It is clear that I still have work to do to get back on the line. After breaking 3 hours at age 45, I wanted to do it one more time, but the age factors now tell me that this is out of the question. It is also the same thing my kids are telling me.

These personal rumblings should give an idea of how you can use the age factors in Table 8-4. As a rough rule of thumb, you can think of yourself as slowing down from age 35 at a rate of about 0.6 percent per year until about age 60. In your 60s the rate increases from about 1.0 percent per year to 2.0 percent per year, and in your 70s the rate increases from about 2.0 percent per year to 3.0 percent per year.

Other Results

World records by age exist for many events besides the marathon, and lines like that in Figure 8-1 have been estimated for some of them. The slowdown rate, transition age, and increase in the slowdown rate do differ somewhat across events. Table 8-5 presents results based on a line that was determined using observations for the middle distances: 400, 800, 1,500, 3,000, 5,000, and 10,000 meters. The transition age, the slowdown rate, and the increase in the slowdown rate were assumed to be the same for these six events, but obviously each had its own separate intercept. The transition age was 59.5, almost exactly the same as 59.6 for the marathon. The slowdown rate before the transition age was 0.81 percent, somewhat higher than the 0.62 for the marathon. On the

TABLE **8-5** Age-Graded Factors for Middle Distances

Age	Age-Graded Factor	Percentage Change in Factor	Age	Age-Graded Factor	Percentage Change in Factor
35	1.000	0.81	68	1.337	1.31
36	1.008	0.81	69	1.355	1.37
37	1.016	0.81	70	1.374	1.43
38	1.025	0.81	71	1.395	1.49
39	1.033	0.81	72	1.416	1.55
40	1.041	0.81	73	1.439	1.60
41	1.050	0.81	74	1.463	1.66
42	1.058	0.81	75	1.488	1.72
43	1.067	0.81	76	1.515	1.78
44	1.075	0.81	77	1.543	1.84
45	1.084	0.81	78	1.572	1.90
46	1.093	0.81	79	1.602	1.95
47	1.102	0.81	80	1.635	2.01
48	1.111	0.81	81	1.669	2.07
49	1.120	0.81	82	1.704	2.13
50	1.129	0.81	83	1.741	2.19
51	1.138	0.81	84	1.780	2.25
52	1.147	0.81	85	1.822	2.30
53	1.156	0.81	86	1.865	2.36
54	1.166	0.81	87	1.910	2.42
55	1.175	0.81	88	1.957	2.48
56	1.185	0.81	89	2.007	2.54
57	1.194	0.81	90	2.059	2.60
58	1.204	0.81	91	2.113	2.65
59	1.214	0.81	92	2.171	2.71
60	1.224	0.85	93	2.231	2.77
61	1.235	0.91	94	2.294	2.83
62	1.247	0.96	95	2.360	2.89
63	1.260	1.02	96	2.430	2.95
64	1.273	1.08	97	2.503	3.00
65	1.288	1.14	98	2.579	3.06
66	1.303	1.20	99	2.660	3.12
67	1.319	1.26	100	2.744	3.18

other hand, the increase in the slowdown rate was 0.06, considerably smaller than the 0.12 for the marathon.

These results thus tell us that in comparing the middle distances to the marathon, the slowdown rate is larger initially but does not increase as fast after the transition age. This does not seem unreasonable. You might expect that the ability to do a really hard job, like running a marathon, deteriorates more rapidly at older ages than does an easier, less time-consuming job, like running 1,500 meters (my apologies to 1,500-meter runners). The larger slowdown rates for the early ages may mean that speed deteriorates faster than endurance. A rule of thumb for the middle distances is that you slow down by about 0.8 percent per year until age 60. Between age 60 and 70 the slowdown rate increases to about 1.5 percent per year, and between age 70 and 80 it increases to about 2.0 percent.

If we stop at age 90 in Tables 8-4 and 8-5, which is probably about as far as the tables should be pushed, the age factor for the marathon is 2.522 versus 2.059 for the middle distances, a difference of about 22 percent. Table 8-5 results are thus even more optimistic than those of Table 8-4 regarding deterioration rates. The age factor for age 75, for example, is only 27 percent larger than the age factor for age 55. Someone age 85 is only 82 percent slower than he or she was at age 35.

Although world-record times do not exist for many physical activities, such as mowing the lawn with a hand mower, shoveling snow, bagging groceries, and so forth, it seems likely that the slowdown rates for these activities do not differ greatly from the rates in either Table 8-4 or Table 8-5. Which table you should use depends on the length of the activity. If you have a large lawn that takes four or five hours to hand mow, use the marathon table; otherwise use the middle-distance table. The tables may be useful guides to much of your physical life.

The results in Tables 8-4 and 8-5 are based on data only for men, but the data are probably a fairly good guide for women as well. It is hard to estimate a line like that in Figure 8-1 using world records for women because the small sample problem is severe for women. For example, very few women in their 60s and 70s have run a marathon, and for many ages it is unlikely we are getting times near the biological limit. Probably the best we can do for now is to assume that the men's results pertain to women as well.

A common measure of aerobic capacity in physiology is known as VO_{2max} (we will not discuss here how this is measured). It is well known that VO_{2max} declines with age, but unfortunately there is nothing in the physiological literature for VO_{2max} that is equivalent to Tables 8-4 or 8-5. The VO_{2max} results that are available so far thus do not provide much of a check on the results using world records. An interesting question for future work, however, is whether VO_{2max} results can be used to help estimate slowdown rates, especially for the very old ages.

Conclusion

We have used our statistical tools—primarily choosing a best fitting line subject to a restriction—to estimate how people physically deteriorate with age. As discussed above, these results may be of interest to policy makers in deciding how to treat the aging. But then again it may be that the age factors in Tables 8-4 and 8-5 are of interest only to old runners as they run ever more slowly into the sunset.

9 Interest Rates

This is a song to celebrate banks,
Because they are full of money and you go into them and all
    you hear is clinks and clanks,
Or maybe a sound like the wind in the trees on the hills,
Which is the rustling of the thousand dollar bills.
Most bankers dwell in marble halls,
Which they get to dwell in because they encourage deposits
    and discourage withdrawals,
And particularly because they all observe one rule which woe
    betides the banker who fails to heed it,
Which is you must never lend any money to anybody unless
    they don't need it.

Ogden Nash, from Bankers Are Just Like Anybody Else,
Except Richer

There is a lot of macroeconomics in this chapter and the next, a subject that is not everyone's cup of tea. This chapter discusses interest rates, and the next one discusses inflation. Interest rates are something you should be excited about because they have important effects on people's lives. We will see that Alan Greenspan, the chairman of the Federal Reserve (the Fed), plays an important role in the story in this chapter. He is considered one of the most powerful people in the world. So please read on. Macroeconomics is more exciting than you might think.

There are many kinds of interest rates. If you have a savings account in a bank, you earn interest at the interest rate that the bank pays. If you have a mortgage, you pay interest at the mortgage rate you agreed to when you took out the mortgage. If you buy a corporate bond, you earn interest at the corporate bond rate. Some interest rates are for a short period of time, such as three months or a year. Other interest rates are longer term. A mortgage rate may be for 20 to 30 years, and a corporate bond rate may be for 10 to 15 years.

The interest rate that we are concerned with in this chapter is for a period of three months, and it is called the three-month Treasury bill rate. Part of the debt of the U.S. government is in the form of three-month securities, and it is the interest rate on these securities that we will explain. For shorthand, we will call the three-month Treasury bill rate the *bill rate*.

Now things get more interesting. How is the bill rate determined? For all intents and purposes, it is determined by Alan Greenspan, the current chairman of the Fed. About every six weeks the Federal Open Market Committee (FOMC) of the Federal Reserve meets to set the value of the interest rate. The interest rate that the Fed actually controls is called the *federal funds rate,* which is an overnight interest rate at which commercial banks borrow and lend to each other. The Fed controls this rate by buying and selling government securities in the private market. The chairman of the Fed has enormous influence in the FOMC meetings, and it is extremely rare for the FOMC to do something that the chairman does not want to do. At the current time (the year 2001) Alan Greenspan is clearly running the show.

When the Fed changes the federal funds rate, other interest rates change as well. There is almost a one for one change in the three-month Treasury bill rate, and because of this, we will assume in this chapter that the Fed also controls the bill rate. Although not necessarily one for one, changes in the federal funds rate also lead to changes in interest rates like those on savings accounts, corporate bonds, and mortgages. Interest rates in other countries also generally change when U.S. interest rates change. The decision that the Fed makes every six weeks about the federal funds rate thus has an effect on many interest rates.

Why are interest rates a big deal? This chapter is not a primer on macroeconomics, but a few things should be said about the effects of interest rates on the economy. First, interest rates have an effect on stock prices. If you follow the stock market, you know that market analysts hang on every word that Greenspan says, looking for clues as to whether he will raise or lower interest rates in the future. Generally high interest rates are bad for stock prices, and low interest rates are good.

Second, interest rates affect the demand for housing. If mortgage rates are high, it is costly to borrow money to buy a new house, and fewer people choose to do so. Fewer new houses are then built.

Third, interest rates also affect the demand for large items like cars and refrigerators. If interest rates are high, it is again costly to borrow money to buy these items, and fewer people choose to do so.

Fourth, interest rates affect the plant and equipment investment of firms. If interest rates are high, it is costly for firms to borrow money to finance new investment projects, and fewer investment projects are undertaken.

Finally, interest rates affect consumer spending through their effect on stock prices. Households own stocks, and when stock prices rise, household wealth rises. A fraction of this increase in wealth is spent by households each year, so a rise in wealth leads to a rise in consumer spending. A fall in interest rates can thus stimulate consumer spending by first stimulating stock prices. Conversely, a rise in interest rates causes consumer spending to decrease by first depressing stock prices.

All this means that an increase in interest rates has a negative effect on expenditures on consumer goods, expenditures on housing, and investment in plant and equipment. Conversely, a decrease in interest rates has a positive effect. Fed policy thus has an important influence on the economy. Since the U.S. economy affects the economies of other countries, Fed policy also has an influence on these economies as well.

I hope this discussion has given you a sense that Fed policy is important in everyone's economic life. The aim of this chapter, however, is not to explain the effects of Fed policy on the economy. Rather, we are interested in what motivates the Fed to do what it does. Just as we have tried to explain the behavior of voters regarding votes for president and the behavior of married individuals regarding how much time (if any) to spend in an affair, we will try to explain the behavior of the Fed. Why does the Fed at times raise interest rates and at other times lower them? If we can explain this behavior, we can then use the results to predict what the Fed will do in the future. As usual, we begin with a theory, move to the data, test, think about pitfalls, examine the results, and then predict.

A Theory of Fed Behavior

It is no secret that monetary authorities around the world, including the Fed, hate inflation. One of the main goals of any monetary authority is to keep inflation in check, and for some monetary authorities—although not the Fed—this is the only goal. How does the Fed try to keep inflation in check? We discuss inflation in the next chapter, where we will see that inflation is affected by demand pressure in the economy. Other things being equal, when overall demand in the economy rises, inflation rises, and when overall demand falls, inflation falls. Since the Fed affects overall demand by changing interest rates, it also indirectly affects inflation because demand affects inflation. Therefore, if inflation is higher than the Fed would like, the Fed can raise interest rates to bring inflation down. Inflation is thus likely to have an effect on the Fed's interest setting behavior.

The Fed, however, cares about things other than inflation. One thing in particular it cares about is unemployment. If unemployment is high, many people are looking for a job and cannot find one, which is not a good thing. The Fed can lower unemployment by lowering interest rates, thus stimulating overall demand. If demand increases, the total output produced in the economy increases, and this in turn increases employment because workers are needed to produce the additional output. Thus the unemployment rate is likely to have an effect on the Fed's interest setting behavior. If the unemployment rate is higher than the Fed would like, it can lower interest rates to bring unemployment down.

If this theory is right, the bill rate (which the Fed for all intents and purposes controls) should depend on inflation and the unemployment rate. Is there anything else? We will see that there are other variables that appear to affect Fed behavior, but the main two are clearly inflation and the unemployment rate. If you remember just these two, you know most of what influences Fed behavior.

The Fed is also concerned about the growth of the money supply. (The *money supply* is roughly the amount of cash in circulation and the amount in checking accounts.) If the money supply has been growing rapidly in the past, the Fed may fear that this will lead to inflation in the future. In other words, the Fed may care about past money supply growth because it cares about future inflation. The past growth of the money supply may thus have a positive effect on the interest rate that the Fed sets. For example, a large past growth of the money supply may lead the Fed to raise interest rates.

There is a period in U.S. history in which the Fed, chaired by Paul Volcker, announced that it was mostly concerned about the money supply. Volcker was chair of the Fed between the third quarter of 1979 and the second quarter of 1987, and the period for which the money supply policy was in effect is the fourth quarter of 1979 through the third quarter of 1982. This period will be called the *early Volcker period*. We would expect the money supply variable to have more of an effect on the bill rate in this period than either before or after, and we will see that this is the case.

A key characteristic of Fed behavior is a tendency to change interest rates in small steps. If, for example, the Fed is in the process of raising interest rates, it often does this by raising the federal funds rate by 0.25 percent each time the FOMC meets (about every six weeks). The Fed does not appear to like large, abrupt changes in interest rates. This means that the value of the federal funds rate at the time of the meeting has an important effect on the new rate that is set. This is, of course, obvious. If when the Fed makes a change the size of the change is typically small, then the rate at the time of the meeting has a large effect on the new rate. The Fed's interest setting behavior is thus influenced by the value of the existing rate at the time of the meeting.

There are two timing issues that are relevant for the question of how fast the Fed changes interest rates. First, we will see that the *change* in the unemployment rate appears to affect Fed behavior. If, for example, the unemployment rate is rising, the Fed appears to lower interest rates, other things being equal. In other words, although the Fed tends to change interest rates in small steps, it seems to decrease interest rates faster when the unemployment rate is rising and increase interest rates faster when the unemployment rate is falling.

The other timing issue concerns past changes in interest rates. The change in the bill rate last quarter and the change in the quarter before that appear to affect the Fed's current choice of the rate. We will not say much about these timing issues. They are not the most important feature of Fed behavior, which is the Fed's concern with inflation and unemployment, but we will see that the timing variables are significant.

The theory is summarized in Box 9-1. *Lagged* means that the variable is the value for the previous quarter, and *lagged twice* means that the variable is the value for the quarter before that. The variable *money growth lagged—early Volcker* is equal to money growth lagged during

bill rate depends on:	
	inflation
	unemployment rate
	change in unemployment rate
	money growth lagged
	money growth lagged—early Volcker
	bill rate lagged
	change in bill rate lagged
	change in bill rate lagged twice

the early Volcker period and zero otherwise. Putting in a separate variable for this period is a way of accounting for the different behavior during the early Volcker period.

The Data

The data that we need to test the theory are easy to come by. The government compiles data on inflation, the unemployment rate, the money supply, and the bill rate. We will use quarterly data, and the period we consider is the first quarter of 1954 through the third quarter of 1999. There are 183 quarters within this period, so we have 183 observations.

The data on the unemployment rate and inflation are plotted in Figure 9-1. You can see that inflation was high from the mid-1970s through the early 1980s. (We will examine what caused this in the next chapter.) The unemployment rate was also generally high in this period, as well as in 1958, 1961, and the early 1990s.

The bill rate is plotted in Figure 9-2. If you compare Figure 9-1 to Figure 9-2, you can see that the bill rate is generally high when inflation is high, which is consistent with the Fed trying to fight inflation by raising interest rates. After inflation came down in the early 1980s, the Fed lowered the bill rate substantially, an action that is consistent with the Fed trying to bring down the unemployment rate by lowering interest rates.

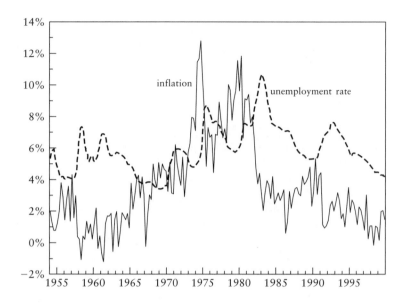

FIGURE **9-1** The Unemployment Rate and Inflation 1954:1–1999:3

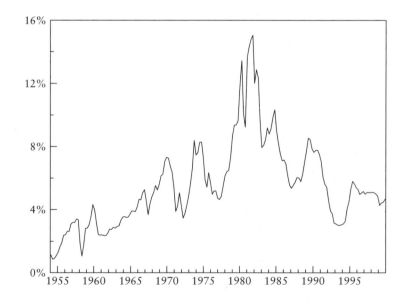

FIGURE **9-2** The Bill Rate 1954:1–1999:3

We also collected data on the money supply, but since the money supply plays a fairly minor role in the story except for the early Volcker period, we will not present a plot of it.

Fit and Test

Given the data, we can use the computer to find the set of coefficients that leads to the smallest sum of squared errors. For each set tried, there are 183 errors, so a lot of computation is going on. Before we begin the computations, however, there is one new complication we need to discuss. The theory says that inflation and the unemployment rate affect the bill rate. That is, the Fed changes the bill rate when inflation and the unemployment rate change. However, as we briefly discussed above, the bill rate also affects inflation and the unemployment rate. For example, when interest rates rise, other things being equal, inflation falls and the unemployment rate rises. We thus have causality in both directions. If we don't do anything about this problem, the best fitting set of coefficients will be biased. Before we use the inflation variable we need to "purge" the effects of the bill rate on it. Likewise, we need to purge the unemployment rate (and the change in the unemployment rate) from the effects of the bill rate on it. The purged variables can then legitimately be used in explaining the bill rate because their variation is not affected by variations in the bill rate. The results below are based on a method that does this purging. The set of coefficients chosen by this method is based on getting a best fit, so the insights from Chapter 2 are still relevant. It is just that the best fit in this case is a little different. It is the one that leads to the smallest sum of squared errors using the purged variables as explanatory variables. (As was the case for the method used in Chapter 5, it is beyond the scope of this book to discuss the details of this method.)

The results are shown in Box 9-2. Inflation has a t-statistic of 4.17, the unemployment rate has a t-statistic of -4.18, and the change in the unemployment rate has a t-statistic of -6.05. The three variables are significant. This is thus strong evidence that the Fed looks at inflation and the unemployment rate in setting interest rates.

The coefficient of money growth lagged for other than the early Volcker period is 0.014 with a t-statistic of 2.26. For the early Volcker period the additional coefficient is 0.219 with a t-statistic of 9.71. The total

BOX **9-2**

bill rate depends on:		t-statistic
0.071	inflation	4.17
−0.131	unemployment rate	−4.18
−0.748	change in unemployment rate	−6.05
0.014	money growth lagged	2.26
0.219	money growth lagged—early Volcker	9.71
0.916	bill rate lagged	47.32
0.210	change in bill rate lagged	3.75
−0.345	change in bill rate lagged twice	−6.71
0.855	intercept	5.42
standard error: 0.47		
number of observations: 183		

coefficient for the early Volcker period is thus the sum of these two, or 0.233. These coefficients are strong evidence that the Fed put more weight on money growth in the early Volcker period than it has otherwise, a result that is consistent with what the Fed actually said it was doing.

The coefficient for the bill rate lagged is 0.916 with a t-statistic of 47.32, which is strong evidence that the Fed adjusts slowly. As previously discussed, the two changes in bill rate pick up timing effects. They have t-statistics of 3.75 and −6.71, respectively, so the two terms are significant.

The standard error is 0.47, which is moderate. It says that 68.2 percent of the time the error in predicting the bill rate should be between −0.47 and 0.47. The highest and lowest values of the bill rate for the 183 observations are 15.09 and 0.81, and 0.47 is quite small relative to this range. On the other hand, the average change in the bill rate from quarter to quarter is 0.49, so the standard error is only slightly smaller than the average quarterly change. There are clearly other factors that affect Fed behavior than the variables we have used. We will say more about this later. The main conclusion to be drawn from the results is that inflation and the unemployment rate have highly significant effects on Fed behavior.

Possible Pitfalls

This first part of this section is hard, and it can be skipped if desired. An important possible pitfall in the social sciences is that people's behavior can change over time in ways that are not accounted for by the theory. When this happens, we say that behavior is not *stable* over time. There are, fortunately, ways of testing whether behavior is stable, and these ways are the subject matter of the first part of this section.

Stability Tests

Probably the main possible pitfall to worry about in this chapter is whether Fed behavior is different now than it was in the 1950s, the 1960s, and the 1970s. We have seen that the Fed's behavior was different in the early Volcker period, and it is possible that its behavior after this period was different from what it was before this period. Remember that the early Volcker period is the fourth quarter of 1979 through the third quarter of 1982. We will use the notation *1979:4* to refer to the fourth quarter of 1979, *1982:3* to refer to the third quarter of 1982, and so on. The early Volcker period is thus 1979:4–1982:3.

Let's consider how we can test whether Fed behavior has changed. We will focus on the period before the early Volcker period, which is 1954:1–1979:3, and the period after the early Volcker period, which is 1982:4–1999:3. We will call these two periods the *first* and *second* periods. The middle period (that is, what we've called the *early Volcker period*) is excluded; we know that Fed behavior was different in this period because the Fed said so. If Fed behavior is different between the first and second periods, then we will find that at least some of the coefficients are different between the two periods.

How can we test whether the coefficients are different? The main idea is to compare two measures of fit. The first measure is the smallest sum of squared errors that is obtained when we combine the first and second periods. In other words, we find the best fitting set of coefficients using all the observations in the two periods. We will call this *measure one*. For the second measure we treat the two periods separately. We find the best fitting set of coefficients using only observations for the first period and then the best fitting set of coefficients using only observations for the second period. Each of these two sets has associated with it a sum of squared errors for the respective period, and if we add these two sums we get our second measure of fit, which we will call *measure two*.

Now comes a key point: measure two will always be smaller than measure one. We are allowed more flexibility in fitting the data for measure two because we can fit the two periods separately. Measure one forces us to use the same set of coefficients for both periods, but measure two does not. Now, if the true set of coefficients is in fact the same in the two periods (that is, Fed behavior has not changed from the first to the second period), measure two should be only slightly smaller than measure one. On the other hand, if the true set of coefficients is different in the second period than in the first, measure two is likely to be much smaller than measure one. In this case measure one is incorrectly forced to use a common set of coefficients for both periods, and the fit should not be very good. Therefore, if measure one is much larger than measure two, this suggests that behavior has changed.

We are not done, however, because we need some way to decide when the difference between measures one and two is large and when it is not. Here we need to go back to thinking about different universes, as we did in Chapter 2. Assume that Fed behavior has not changed and that the results in Box 9-2 are correct. We know that the size of a typical error is the standard error, which is given in the box as 0.47. If we assume that the errors come from a bell-shaped curve with a standard error of 0.47, we can draw different errors for our second universe, which gives us different bill rate values. The second universe differs from the first in having different bill rate values, but everything else is the same. In particular, Fed behavior has not changed in the second universe because we are using Box 9-2, which assumes unchanged Fed behavior. This drawing is similar to the one we discussed in Lesson 4 in Chapter 2 in the sense that we are getting a second universe with different errors and thus different values of the bill rate. For this second universe, we can compute measure one and measure two and then the difference between the two. The results will be different than they were in our first universe (that is, the actual universe) because we are using different values of the bill rate.

Imagine doing this 1,000 times for 1,000 universes. In the end we will have computed 1,000 differences between measures one and two. The next step is to put these differences in order of their size, starting from the largest. Remember that these differences have all been computed under the assumption that there has been no change in Fed behavior.

We are now almost done. Given the actual data that we have (from our current universe), we can compute measures one and two and then the difference between them. We can see how this difference in the actual data compares to the 1,000 differences we have computed and ordered by size. Say that the difference in the actual data is between differences 150 and 151. This says that if the truth is no change in behavior (that is, no change in the coefficients from the first period to the second), we could expect to get a difference as large as ours about 15 percent of the time (150 out of 1000). This percent is greater than the usual cutoff of 5 percent, so we would accept the view that there has been no change in behavior. If, on the other hand, the difference in the actual data was between differences 10 and 11, we would reject the view of no change. In this case we would expect to get a difference that large only about 1 percent of the time, which is smaller than the 5 percent cutoff.

In practice, stability tests are a little more complicated than this, and the tests can be done without having to draw errors for other universes. The intuition is, however, the same. The view of no change in behavior (stable behavior) is rejected if the difference in fit (that is, the difference between measures like one and two) is large compared to what one would expect to get if the truth were no change.

I used a stability test to test whether there was a change in Fed behavior between the first and second periods, and the case of no change in behavior was not rejected. The computed difference between the two measures (measures like one and two) was such that we could expect to get a value as large as that about 19 percent of the time. The case of no change in Fed behavior is thus not rejected because 19 percent is greater than the cutoff of 5 percent. The results from the test thus support the view that Fed behavior has not changed since 1954 except for the early Volcker period.

Unemployment Rate Versus Output Gap

Another possible pitfall concerns the use of the unemployment rate as an explanatory variable. A similar measure of how well the economy is doing is the *output gap*. The output gap is the difference between potential output and actual output. Potential output is an estimate of how much output the economy could produce if there were full employment. The unemployment rate and the output gap are obviously closely related, since unemployment tends to fall as actual output gets closer to potential. In practice, however, the unemployment rate and the output gap are not perfectly related, and the Fed may look at the output gap and not the unemployment rate when setting the interest rate. If this were true, it is likely that the unemployment rate would be significant in explaining the bill rate (which it is) because it would be serving as a proxy for the output gap. We would, of course, be making a mistake because it would actually be the output gap that the Fed is looking at.

We can easily test for the output gap versus the unemployment rate by adding the output gap as an explanatory variable and testing to see if it is significant. If the Fed actually looks at the output gap and not the unemployment rate, the output gap should be significant and the unemployment rate should not be significant when both are included as explanatory variables. In fact, when the output gap was included, it was not significant, and the unemployment rate remained significant. These results thus favor the use of the unemployment rate over the output gap. The same conclusion was reached when the variables for the change in the output gap and the change in the unemployment rate were compared. When both variables were added, the change in the output gap was not significant and the change in the unemployment rate was.

As discussed in Chapter 2, when deciding between two possible explanatory variables, a common procedure is to run a horse race. If one variable has a t-statistic that is greater than 2.0 or less than -2.0 and the other does not, the first variable wins. In this case the race was between the unemployment rate and the output gap, and the unemployment rate won.

Examine the Results

We can now use our results to see how much the Fed is predicted to change the bill rate when inflation changes. Say that inflation increased by 1 percentage point (from, say, 3 percent to 4 percent). How much would the bill rate be predicted to increase? The coefficient for inflation in Box 9-2 is 0.071, so the increase in the first quarter would be 0.071 (from, say, 5.0 percent to 5.071 percent). This does not seem that large, but we are not done. Remember that the Fed tends to move slowly, as reflected in the large coefficient of 0.916 for the bill rate lagged. Given that the change in the first quarter was 0.071, the change in the second quarter (from the already higher first quarter value) is 0.916 times 0.071, or .065. The change in the third quarter is 0.916 times 0.065, or 0.060, and so on through as many quarters as we want to consider. If we add all the changes (0.071, 0.065, 0.060, and so on), we get 0.85. Therefore, in the long run the bill rate changes by 0.85 percentage points when inflation changes by 1.0 percentage point. (Actually, the changes after the initial 0.071 change in the first quarter are not quite 0.065, 0.060, and so on, because the change in the bill rate variables have an effect, but the long-run change is 0.85.)

We can also use our results to see how much the Fed is predicted to change the bill rate when the unemployment rate changes. Say that the unemployment rate rises by 1 percentage point (from, say, 4 percent to 5 percent). How much would the bill rate decrease? The coefficient for the unemployment rate is −0.131 and the coefficient for the change in the unemployment rate is −0.748. The decrease in the bill rate in the first quarter would thus be 0.131 plus 0.748, or 0.879. The results thus say that if the unemployment rate did rise in one quarter by 1 percentage point, which is a large increase in one quarter, the Fed would aggressively respond by lowering the bill rate in the quarter by 0.879 percentage points. The long-run change in the bill rate is harder to calculate for an unemployment rate change than for an inflation rate change because the unemployment rate appears in both level and change form, but this can be done. I did the calculation, and the long-run decrease in the bill rate in response to a 1 percentage point increase in the unemployment rate is 1.56 percentage points. The Fed is thus predicted to be fairly aggressive in fighting unemployment.

Another way to examine the results is to see what they imply about Fed behavior over the entire period (from 1954 through 1999). This is done in Figure 9-3, which shows the predicted values of the bill rate using the actual values of inflation, the unemployment rate, and the money supply. Nine subperiods are shown in the figure. These represent periods in which the actual values differ from the predicted values by noticeable amounts for a number of consecutive quarters. There is one

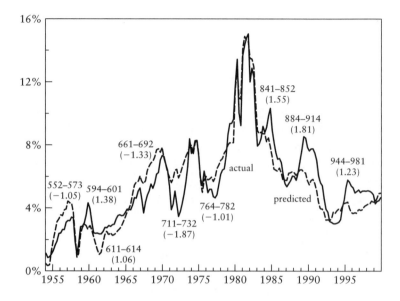

FIGURE **9-3** Actual and Predicted Values of the Bill Rate 1954:1–1999:3
Notes: Values in parentheses are average errors for each of the subperiods.
The notation 552–573 means 1955:2–1957:3.

subperiod in the early 1960s in which the bill rate was noticeably higher than predicted, and there are three subperiods from the mid-1980s and later in which this was true. The bill rate was noticeably lower than predicted in the mid-1950s, two subperiods in the 1960s, and two subperiods in the 1970s. Figure 9-3 shows in parentheses the average error for each of the nine subperiods.

One way of thinking about the errors in Figure 9-3 is the following. Each time the Fed makes a decision at an FOMC meeting, it knows more than is reflected in the variables that have been used in this chapter. That is, it knows more than simply the values of inflation, the unemployment rate, and the money supply. The errors can thus be interpreted as the Fed's use of more information than the theory has used to get the predicted values. For example, the Fed has information on the stock market, which is not a variable in the box, so one reason for the positive errors in the 1994:4–1998:1 period in Figure 9-3 may have been the Fed's concern about a possible stock market bubble (although there is no sign that the Fed's policy in this period actually slowed the stock market down!).

Predict Fed Behavior

As mentioned above, stock market analysts hang on every word Alan Greenspan says, hoping for clues as to what he will do in the future regarding interest rates. We can, however, make a prediction as to what Greenspan will do without having to follow him around looking for clues. Given an assumption about inflation and an assumption about the unemployment rate, the set of coefficients can be used to predict the bill rate, that is, to predict Fed behavior.

The following example shows how this is done. Assume we are in the last day of the third quarter of 1999 (September 30, 1999). We know (or have good estimates of) the growth of the money supply in the third quarter, the bill rate for the third quarter, the changes in the bill rate for the second and third quarters, and the unemployment rate for the third quarter. We want to predict what the bill rate will be in the fourth quarter of 1999. We have everything we need except the values of inflation and the unemployment rate for the fourth quarter of 1999. If we make assumptions about these two values, we can predict the bill rate.

Box 9-3 calculates the prediction of the bill rate for the fourth quarter of 1999 using a value of 1.84 for inflation and 4.09 for the unemployment rate.

You can see that the bill rate is predicted to be 4.90. This is the predicted value for the fourth quarter of 1999. The actual value of the bill rate for the previous quarter (the third quarter of 1999) was 4.65, so this prediction is for the bill rate to rise by 0.25 percentage points. We have made this prediction without knowing anything about what Greenspan might have been saying at the time.

How accurate is the prediction of 4.90 percent? As shown in the box, the actual value of the bill rate in the fourth quarter of 1999 was 5.04. The error is thus −0.14 percentage points. This error is small compared to the standard error of 0.47, and in this sense the prediction is quite good. The values that were used for the explanatory variables in the box, including the values for inflation and the unemployment rate, are the actual values, and so the prediction of the bill rate is an after-the-fact prediction. Since this is the type of prediction that is relevant for testing theories, the small error using this prediction provides support for the theory. It is not, however, a prediction that could have been made in

BOX **9-3**

coef.	value	coef. × value	
0.071	1.84	0.131	inflation
−0.131	4.09	−0.536	unemployment rate
−0.748	−0.12	0.090	change in unemployment rate
0.014	5.11	0.072	money growth lagged
0.219	0.0	0.0	money growth lagged—early Volcker
0.916	4.65	4.259	bill rate lagged
0.210	0.20	0.042	change in bill rate lagged
−0.345	0.05	−0.017	change in bill rate lagged twice
0.855	1.0	0.855	intercept
		4.90	TOTAL (predicted)
		5.04	Actual
		−0.14	Error

real time because the actual values for inflation and the unemployment rate would not have been known at the time the prediction was made.

In many cases we are interested in predictions more than one quarter ahead. In the present example we might also be interested in the prediction of the bill rate for the first quarter of 2000. Given that we have made a prediction for the fourth quarter of 1999, we can easily make one for the first quarter of 2000. We need to make assumptions about the values of inflation and the unemployment rate for the first quarter of 2000, and we need to make an assumption about the growth rate of the money supply for the fourth quarter of 1999. Given these three values, and given what we have predicted the bill rate to be in the fourth quarter of 1999, we can predict the bill rate for the first quarter of 2000. We can then predict the second quarter of 2000, and so on. The prediction of the bill rate for each quarter uses the prediction from the previous quarter, so the predictions build on themselves.

To give another example, say at the beginning of 2000 you thought that inflation was going to increase substantially in the future because the economy was overheated. If you used the coefficients in Box 9-2 along with large future values of inflation to predict future values of the bill rate, your prediction would be for a substantial increase in the bill rate in the future. You would be predicting a forceful Alan Greenspan trying to combat inflation, and you would have numbers (the bill rate predictions) regarding how forceful he would be.

One more example. Say at the beginning of 2001 you thought that unemployment was going to increase substantially during the year because the U.S. economy was finally going to take a breather from its record expansion. If you used the coefficients in Box 9-2 along with large future values of the unemployment rate to predict future values of the bill rate, your prediction would be for a substantial decrease in the bill rate in the future. You would be predicting a forceful Alan Greenspan trying to fight unemployment by lowering interest rates. Sound familiar? (The Fed lowered the interest rate substantially in 2001 as the unemployment rate rose.)

Since inflation plays a key role in this story, it would be nice to know how inflation is determined. Can we predict inflation? The answer is yes, and we'll see how in the next chapter.

10   Inflation

[Yes, I know, there is no poem. But try finding a good poem on inflation. Inflation does not seem to be high on the list of poets' interests.]

We saw in Chapter 3 that inflation has an effect on voting behavior. If inflation is high at election time, voters tend to vote against the incumbent party, other things being equal. We saw in the last chapter that the Fed raises interest rates when inflation is high to try to bring it down. Inflation has some powerful enemies.

In this chapter we are concerned with trying to explain what determines inflation. Why is it sometimes high, as it was in much of the 1970s, and why is it sometimes low, as it was in the late 1990s? We proceed in the usual way: propose a theory, collect data, use the data to test the theory, think about pitfalls, examine the results, and make a prediction.

We should first be precise about what we mean by inflation. We begin with a measure of the overall price level in the economy. The government computes a number of measures of the overall price level. Some of the more popular ones are (1) the consumer price index, (2) the producer price index, (3) a price index for the total output of the economy (GDP), and (4) a price index for the output of all firms in the economy (this excludes government output). A price index is sometimes called a price level. The percentage change in a price index—that is, how much the price index changes from one period to the next in percentage terms—is called inflation. Inflation is thus the percentage change in some measure of an overall price level. For purposes of this chapter we will use the fourth price index listed above, namely the price index for the output of all firms in the economy.

We will present a theory of how firms set prices. We will then use this theory to consider the likely effects on the overall price level. If we explain the overall price level, we also explain inflation, since inflation is just the percentage change in the overall price level.

A Theory of Price Setting Behavior

Let's begin by considering a single firm producing a single good. Some firms have no control over the price of their goods. A wheat farmer, for example, has no control over the price of wheat. The farmer can sell as much wheat as he or she wants at the current price. If the farmer would like to charge a higher price for the wheat, tough luck. He or she would sell no wheat. On the other hand, the price does not fall if the farmer sells more wheat.

Many firms have some control over the price that they charge for their goods, and these are the firms we are interested in. If this type of firm raises its price, it will sell fewer items, but the demand will not fall to zero, as it does for the wheat farmer. If the firm wants to sell more items, it must lower its price. We thus have a firm that can change the number of items that it sells by changing its price. We are interested in what influences the firm's choice of its price.

A common assumption in economics is that firms maximize profits—they make choices that lead to their profits being as high as possible given the constraints that they face. We will make this assumption in this chapter. We will assume that a firm sets its price to maximize its profits. If profits can be increased by raising the price, the firm will do so; conversely, if profits can be increased by lowering the price, the firm will do so.

Let's consider a firm that is producing 50 items and selling them at a price of $10 per item. The firm's revenue is thus $500. Say that it costs $300 to produce the 100 items. The firm's profit is thus $200. Is this the best that the firm can do? To answer this we need to consider what happens if the firm raises or lowers its output by 1 item. If the firm produces 51 items, it must lower the price a little to sell 51 instead of 50. Say that it needs to lower the price to $9.95 per item. Its revenue is then 51 times $9.95, or $507.45. The increase in revenue is thus $7.45. Note that the increase in revenue from selling the extra item is less than the price of the item because the firm has to lower its price to all customers. (We assume that the firm has to charge the same price to everyone.)

Next we must consider what it costs the firm to produce the extra item. We know that it costs $300 to produce 50 items, which is an average of $6 per item. A common assumption in economics is that the cost of producing an additional item rises as the number of items produced rises. If moving from 40 to 41 items costs an additional $5, moving from 41 to 42 items might cost an additional $5.25. Firms are assumed to run into capacity problems as production rises, which are costly. The firm may, for example, have to pay more for overtime work, or it may have to use older machines that cost more to run per hour. So even though the average cost of the 50 items is $6 per item, the cost of producing the 51st item may be more. If, say, the additional cost is $8, it would not pay the firm to produce the extra item because it would receive only $7.45 in additional revenue.

What if the firm produced 49 instead of 50 items? In this case it can raise its price because it is selling one less item. Say that it could raise its price to $10.05. Its revenue is then 49 times $10.05, or $492.45. The decrease in revenue is thus $7.55. Note that the decrease in revenue from selling one less item is not as large as the price of the item because the firm charges the higher price to all customers.

What about cost when the firm lowers production? If the cost per item rises as production rises, then the cost *saving* obviously falls when production falls. If moving from 50 to 51 items costs an additional $8, it may be that moving from 50 to 49 items saves an amount less than $8. Let's assume the cost saving is $7.50. In this case it would not pay the firm to cut production, because revenue would fall by $7.55 and cost would fall by only $7.50.

Given these numbers, our firm is maximizing its profits by producing 50 items. Profits fall if it either raises or lowers production. In general, a firm keeps raising its production (and thus lowering its price) until the extra revenue it receives is less than the extra cost it incurs.

So what? Well, we are now ready to see what changes a firm's pricing behavior. Say there is an increase in the demand for a firm's good. How will the firm respond? If the firm kept its price at $10, it could sell more items, maybe 60. However, producing the extra 10 items would be costly if the cost per item rises as production rises. It would likely pay the firm to produce less than 60 and raise its price. The profit maximizing point might be, for example, where production is 55 items and the price is $11 per item. Again the firm would move to the point where any change in production would lead to a fall in profits.

If demand for the firm's good fell, the opposite would happen. If demand fell and the firm kept its price at $10, it would sell fewer items, maybe 40. However, the cost per additional item is lower when production is lower, and it will likely pay the firm to produce more than 40 and lower its price. The new profit maximizing point might be, for example, where production is 45 items and the price is $9 per item.

We have thus seen that an increase in demand leads the firm to raise its price and a decrease in demand leads the firm to lower its price. This is the first main point of the theory.

The second main point concerns costs. Say that the firm uses oil in producing its good and that the price of oil rises. Assume that demand for the firm's good remains unchanged, so that the firm could still sell 50 items at a price of $10 per item. After the oil price increase, however, 50 units may no longer be the profit maximizing point. Moving from 50 to 49 units now saves more in costs because the cost saving on oil is greater (because of the higher price of oil). It may now be that the cost saving in moving from 50 to 49 is $9.50 rather than $7.50. The firm is thus likely to benefit from lowering its production and raising its price. The new profit maximizing point might be where production is 45 units and the price is $11 per unit.

The opposite happens when the price of oil falls: the firm would increase production and lower its price. The second main point is thus that costs have a positive effect on price: when costs rise the price rises and vice versa.

The last main issue to consider is the speed with which firms respond to changes in demand and costs. We saw in the last chapter that the Fed tends to respond slowly to changes. We captured this idea by using the previous period's bill rate as an explanatory variable. Firms also appear to respond slowly, and we will capture this by using the previous period's price as an explanatory variable.

We now move from a single firm to the whole economy. Using the theory of the price setting behavior of a firm, we will assume that the price level in the economy depends on some measure of demand in the economy and some measure of costs. We will use as the measure of demand the unemployment rate. When the unemployment rate is low, the economy is booming and demand is high. When the unemployment rate is high, the economy is in recession and demand is low. We thus expect that changes in the unemployment rate should have a negative effect on the price level: a decrease in the unemployment rate should lead to a rise in the price level and vice versa.

We will use two variables to measure costs. The first is a measure of the overall price of imports, which we will call the *cost of imports*. This is a price index of all goods that are imported. Many firms use imports in their production processes, and when the cost of imports rises, firms' costs rise. For example, one of the key goods that is imported is oil, and oil is a cost to many firms. The other measure of costs is the average wage rate in the economy, which we will call the *wage rate*. Wages are a key cost to almost all firms, so when wage rates rise, costs rise. We expect from the theory that the cost of imports and the wage rate should have a positive effect on the price level.

We also expect the lagged price level to have an effect on the current price level because firms take time to adjust to new situations.

We need to consider one other issue before summarizing the theory. For the time period we consider, which is from 1954 to 1999, the price level has an upward trend. Other things being equal, the price level tends to increase each period. This is not something that the above theory explains, so to account for this a *trend* variable is added. This is a variable that simply increases by 1 each quarter.

The theory is summarized in Box 10-1.

BOX **10-1**

price level depends on:	
	unemployment rate
	wage rate
	cost of imports
	price level lagged
	trend
	intercept

The Data

As was the case for the theory of Fed behavior in the last chapter, the data that we need in order to test the theory of price setting behavior are easy to come by. The government compiles data on the price level, the unemployment rate, the wage rate, and the cost of imports (the import price level). Remember that the price level is the price index for the output of all firms in the economy. We will use quarterly data, and the period we will consider is the first quarter of 1954 through the fourth quarter of 1999. There are 184 quarters within this period, so we have 184 observations.

In many case in economics, including the present one, we need to consider whether the variables should be used in their natural units or in percentage terms. For variables like the price level, the cost of imports, and the wage rate, it is usually more appropriate to have them in percentage terms. If a firm's initial price is $5 and it decides on a new price of $6, this is a much larger percentage increase than if the initial price is $10 and the new price is $11. The firm is likely thinking more in percentage terms than in absolute terms. We will thus use the price level, the cost of imports, and the wage rate in percentage terms. (This means using the logarithm of each variable, although it is not really necessary to know this. Just think that the three variables are in percentage terms.)

The data on the price level and the cost of imports are plotted in Figure 10-1. The figure shows that there was almost no increase in the cost of imports in the 1950s and 1960s. There were huge increases in the 1970s, due in large part to a sharp rise in the price of oil. The cost of imports fell slightly in the first half of the 1980s, rose slightly in the last half of the 1980s, and did not change much in the 1990s.

The most rapid increase in the price level occurred in the 1970s, which is also the period of the huge increases in the cost of imports. It thus seems likely that the cost of imports has a positive effect on the price level, which is consistent with the theory that costs affect the price setting behavior of firms.

Fit and Test

As always, we use the computer to find the set of coefficients that leads to the smallest sum of squared errors. In this case there are 184

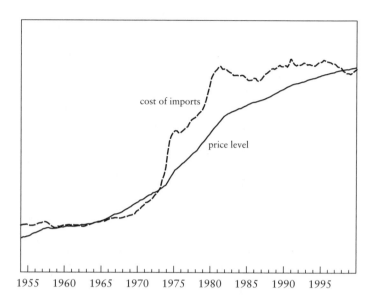

FIGURE **10-1** Price Level and Cost of Imports 1954:1–1999:4

errors for each set of coefficients tried. We have a similar problem here of causality in both directions that we had in the last chapter: the price level affects the unemployment rate and the wage rate, and the unemployment rate and the wage rate affect the price level. We have to purge the effects of the price level on the unemployment rate and the wage rate before we can use them as explanatory variables. We use the same method here as we used in the last chapter. The best fit is the one that leads to the smallest sum of squared errors using the purged variables as explanatory variables.

The results are shown in Box 10-2. The coefficient for the unemployment rate is -0.163 with a t-statistic of -7.09. The unemployment rate is thus significant, and it has a negative effect on the price level: a decrease in the unemployment rate leads to an increase in the price level. The coefficients for the two cost variables, the wage rate and the cost of imports, are 0.053 and 0.048 with t-statistics of 3.45 and 19.98. These variables are also significant, and both have a positive effect on the price level. The significance of the cost of imports is, of course, not surprising given what we know from Figure 10-1.

The coefficient for the price level lagged is 0.870 with a t-statistic of 68.31, which is strong evidence that a firm's price last period has an important effect on the price that it chooses this period.

BOX **10-2**

price level depends on:		t-statistic
−0.163	unemployment rate	−7.09
0.053	wage rate	3.45
0.048	cost of imports	19.98
0.870	price level lagged	68.31
0.031	trend	10.33
−2.29	intercept	−2.02
standard error: 0.32		
number of observations: 184		

The trend variable has a positive coefficient, as expected, and it is significant. This shows that regardless of the other variables, the price level has a positive trend. In other words, there is a tendency for the price level to rise over time independent of anything else.

The standard error is 0.32 percentage points, which is fairly small. It says that 68.2 percent of the time the error in predicting the price level should be between −0.32 and 0.32 percentage points.

Remember that inflation is just the percentage change in the price level, so if we know what affects the price level, we know what affects inflation. We can thus say that the main causes of inflation are demand, as measured by the unemployment rate, and costs, as measured by the cost of imports and the wage rate.

Pitfalls

The results in Box 10-2 have one unreasonable implication, which concerns the size of the effect of a change in the unemployment rate on the price level. The coefficient tells us that a decrease in the unemployment rate of, say, 1 percentage point leads to an increase in the price level of 0.163 percentage points in the first quarter. This 0.163 value is the same regardless of the initial size of the unemployment rate. It does not matter whether the fall of 1 percentage point was from an unemployment rate of 10 percent or of 4 percent. It is not reasonable, however, to assume that the 0.163 value holds for very low values of the unemployment rate.

This point can be seen in Figure 10-2. Case 1 pertains to the present results. Other things being equal, the relationship between the price level and the unemployment rate is represented by a straight line. The slope of the line is constant. Case 2 depicts a situation that seems more reasonable. It says that as the unemployment rate gets closer and closer to a small number, which is assumed to be 2.0 percent in the figure, the price level rises at an increasing rate. In this case lowering the unemployment rate by 1 percentage point has a much larger effect on the price level when the unemployment rate is close to 2 percent than when it is not.

You might ask, why did we use case 1 when case 2 seems more reasonable? The answer is that we don't have enough observations on the curved part of the line in case 2 to determine where the bend in the line starts and how steep it becomes. Most of our observations are for unemployment rates above 4.0 percent. If the line to the right of 4.0 is roughly straight, as drawn in case 2, then all we can do with our observations is determine the slope of the straight line.

What this means is that we cannot use our results to predict with any confidence what would happen to the price level if the unemployment rate falls much below 4.0 percent. We simply have no historical experience to guide us. This is an important pitfall, but one we can do nothing about, except to limit any use of the coefficients to situations in which the unemployment rate is not extremely low. We will come back to this problem at the end of this chapter.

Another possible pitfall relates to the use of the unemployment rate as the measure of demand in the economy. There are many possible measures, and the unemployment rate may not be the best one. One alternative measure is the output gap, which was discussed in the last chapter. Remember that the output gap is the difference between potential output and actual output. We can test the output gap versus the unemployment rate by adding the output gap as an explanatory variable and seeing if it is significant. If the price level responds more to the output gap than to the unemployment rate, the output gap should be significant and the unemployment rate should not be. This is the standard horse race test discussed in Chapter 2. When the output gap was added, it was not significant and the unemployment rate remained significant. These results thus favor the use of the unemployment rate over the output gap. This is the same conclusion that was reached in the last chapter regarding the explanation of the bill rate.

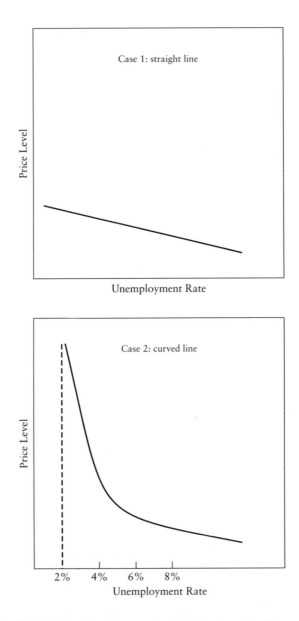

FIGURE **10-2** Possible Relationships Between the Price Level and the Unemployment Rate (other things being equal)

Another possible pitfall concerns the use of the price level lagged as an explanatory variable. Does this variable adequately capture the price adjustment behavior of firms? Perhaps the price level lagged twice should also be an explanatory variable. This was tested by adding the price level lagged twice, and it was not significant. There is thus no evidence on this score that the adjustment process is inadequately captured.

There are many views in economics about the best way to explain inflation, and the present results would not be accepted by everyone as being any good. The idea that demand and costs affect inflation is accepted by nearly everyone. Some of the disagreements are about how to measure demand, but the more important disagreements concern price adjustment issues. Some would argue that the dependent variable should be inflation, not the price level, and some would argue that the dependent variable should be the *change* in inflation. If either of these views is right, the price level lagged twice should be significant when added to the present results. It is not, so this is at least some evidence against these views. This debate is, however, far from over.

Examine the Results and Predict

As discussed in the last section, we should not use the results to examine situations in which the unemployment rate is much below 4.0 percent. You should thus take the following discussion as pertaining only to situations where the unemployment rate remains above about 4.0 percent.

The coefficient for the unemployment rate is −0.163, which says that the price level rises 0.163 percent in the first quarter after a fall in the unemployment rate of 1 percentage point. Because of the effect of the lagged price level, in the next quarter the price level rises .870 times 0.163, or 0.142 percent. In the quarter after that it rises .870 times 0.142, or 0.124 percent, and so on. We can add all these changes up, and if we do so we get a total for the long-run increase in the price level of 1.25 percent. This is, however, a little misleading, since when the price level rises the wage rate is likely to rise, and we have not taken this into account. If we did take the wage rate response into account (which would require results explaining the wage rate), the long-run response would be higher. An increase in the price level leads to an increase in the wage rate, which in turn leads to a further increase in the price level, and so on. We can thus say here that the long-run response of the price level to a fall in the unemployment rate of 1 percentage point is *at least* 1.25 percent.

The coefficient for the cost of imports is 0.048, so an increase in the cost of imports of 10 percent would lead to an increase in the price level of 0.48 percent in the initial quarter. In the next quarter the increase would be 0.870 times 0.48, or 0.42, and so on. The long-run response is (at least) 3.69 percent. This is a fairly large response. It says that in the long run the price level rises by a little over a third of any increase in the cost of imports. Again, Figure 10-1 shows why this effect is estimated to be so large. Large changes in the cost of imports are bad news for policy makers because they have such large effects on the price level.

The coefficient for the wage rate is 0.053, so an increase in the wage rate of 10 percent would lead to an increase in the price level of 0.53 percent in the initial quarter. In the next quarter the increase would be 0.870 times 0.53, or 0.46, and so on. The long run response is 4.08 percent. Again, this is an underestimate because the price level affects the wage rate as well as vice versa. To be more precise we would need to explain the wage rate and then use these results along with the price level results to examine long-run effects.

Just as we predicted the bill rate in the last chapter, we can predict inflation in this chapter. For example, if we are in the last day of 1999, we know or have a good estimate of the price level for the fourth quarter of 1999. If we want to predict what the price level will be in first quarter of 2000, we need to make assumptions about the unemployment rate, the wage rate, and the cost of imports for the first quarter of 2000. If we make assumptions about these three values, we can use the coefficients in Box 10-2 to predict the price level for the first quarter of 2000. The predicted inflation rate is then simply the predicted percentage change in the price level. We can then go on and make a prediction for the second quarter of 2000, and so on.

I will not present any calculations here. The procedure is the same as in the last chapter for the calculations of the bill rate predictions.

Inflation and the Fed

We know from the last chapter that the Fed raises the interest rate when inflation increases. We know from this chapter that inflation increases when the unemployment rate decreases, the cost of imports increases, or the wage rate increases. The Fed also knows this, and it watches closely for signs that labor markets are getting tight, that import costs like oil prices are rising, or that wage rates are rising. At the beginning of 2000 the unemployment rate was low, and oil prices had risen substantially. The Fed was thus concerned that inflation was going to increase, and it raised the interest rate three times between February and May 2000. The total increase was 1 percentage point.

A risk that the Fed faced in 2000 was the possibility that case 2 in Figure 10-2 is true and that the economy was near the point where the line starts to get steep. As long as the economy is on the straight line in case 2, the cost of not tightening enough in terms of an increase in the price level is fairly modest. On the other hand, if the economy is near the bend and the unemployment rate falls into this zone, the increase in the price level could be quite large.

Alas, this is where the tools that have been discussed in this book are of little help. As discussed above, we have too few observations at very low unemployment rates to be able to determine where the bend occurs. In this sense the Fed was groping in the dark in 2000, having little historical experience to guide it. From the point of view of a social scientist, it would have been useful if the economy had moved into the high inflation zone. This would have finally allowed estimates to be made of where the bend begins and how fast the line curves up. Not that we should hope this ever happens. This would be a high price for society to pay for better estimates.

The economy did not in fact go into a high inflation zone in 2000, and by 2001 a significant slowdown had begun. The Fed switched from worrying about inflation to worrying about unemployment. So that's end-of-story about the Fed and inflation for now, but if inflation comes back, Box 9-2 says that the Fed will fight it.

11 More Things

The aim of this book has been to give the nontechnical reader a sense of how social scientists use statistical tools to try to explain behavior. The steps of proposing a theory, collecting data, fitting the data, using the data to test the theory, thinking about pitfalls, examining the results, and making a prediction have been used in each chapter. If the tests do not support the theory or the pitfalls seem serious, the last two steps are not of much interest. We must have some confidence in the results before using them.

One of the main limitations in the social sciences is the availability of good data to test theories. We saw this in the chapter on extramarital affairs, where the two surveys that were used were far from ideal. When thinking about pitfalls, the first question to consider is how good the data are.

This book has only scratched the surface regarding empirical work in the social sciences. A useful type of data that has not been considered is one in which observations are available on many individuals over many time periods. The same people, for example, may have been surveyed once a year for many years. With this type of data it is possible to examine how behavior changes across people as well as across time. The same methodology of theory, data, fitting, testing, and so forth can be used.

A similar type of data is one in which there are observations across states or cities as well as across time. In examining voting behavior, for example, we can get data on votes for president by state. Data are also available across countries as well as across time. For example, observations on interest rates, unemployment rates, and inflation are available for most countries in the world over many years.

Many theories, especially in economics, concern more than one dependent variable at the same time. We briefly mentioned this in the last two chapters. The bill rate affects inflation and the unemployment rate as well as vice versa, and the price level affects the unemployment rate and the wage rate as well as vice versa. As noted in the two chapters, there are statistical methods for dealing with such cases. These methods are best fitting type of methods, so the insights from Chapter 2 are still relevant. The general idea is to find a set of coefficients that fit the data well. Tests are available that are similar to tests using t-statistics. The general testing procedure is to compute the probability that we would get the particular answer we did if our theory is wrong. If the computed probability is low (like a large t-statistic), then the data support the theory, aside from possible pitfall problems.

W. H. Auden aside, I hope this book has given you a deeper appreciation of what social scientists do.

Chapter Notes

Chapter 1

The material in this chapter and in Chapter 3 is taken from a series of papers I did on votes for president. The first one is Ray C. Fair, "The Effect of Economic Events on Votes for President," *The Review of Economics and Statistics* 60 (May 1978), 159–73; the least technical discussion is in Ray C. Fair, "Econometrics and Presidential Elections," *Journal of Economic Perspectives* 10 (June 1996), 89–102; and the latest one is Ray C. Fair, "The Effect of Economic Events on Votes for President: 1996 Update," unpublished, November 6, 1998.

A study that showed that people remember peak stimuli more than average stimuli is Donald A. Redelmeier and Daniel Kahneman, "Patients' Memories of Painful Medical Treatments: Real-Time and Retrospective Evaluations of Two Minimally Invasive Procedures," *Pain* (1996), 3–8. This study showed that people also tend to remember the last part of the experiment more than earlier parts, which is consistent with the use of the growth rate in the year of the election as one of the variables explaining voting behavior.

Chapter 2

I have tried to present the material in this chapter in an intuitive way without saying anything wrong—under the assumption that the errors are normally distributed. To be exact Figure 2-4 should be a *t*-distribution and not a normal distribution, but I have stated in the text that the normal distribution in the figure is only an approximation.

Chapter 3

Regarding the 1924 election, the analysis in David Burner, "Election of 1924" in ed. Arthur M. Schlesinger, Jr., *History of American Presidential Elections 1789–1968*, Volume III, (New York: McGraw-Hill, 1971) 2488, suggests that La Follette may have taken about three-fourths of his votes from the Democrats. The Republicans got 58 percent of the House of Representatives vote in 1924, and the Democrats got 42 percent. Coolidge got 54 percent of the total votes for president, Davis got 29 percent, and La Follette got 17 percent. If it is assumed that Coolidge would have gotten 58 percent if La Follette had not run (the same percentage as the House vote), with Davis getting 42 percent, then La Follette took 23.5 percent ([58 – 54] / 17) from Coolidge and 76.5 percent ([42 – 29] / 17) from Davis. These are the numbers used in Chapter 3.

Chapter 4

The results in this chapter are taken from my Web site: http://fairmodel. econ.yale.edu. The update of the analysis through the 2000 election and real-time predictions for the 2004 election using this update will begin on the Web site in November 2002. The economic model of the United States that was used for the predictions of the economic variables is also on this site. You can use the Web site to make predictions of the 2004 election for different choices of the economic variables.

Chapter 5

The material in this chapter is taken from Ray C. Fair, "A Theory of Extramarital Affairs," *Journal of Political Economy* 86 (February 1978), 45–61. I have stated in the chapter that something that increases the utility from the affair has a positive effect on time spent in the affair. This seems likely, but the effect in the theoretical model is ambiguous—see pages 50–51 of the paper. The ambiguity comes from a subtle income effect. The estimator used is the Tobit estimator; see James Tobin, "Estimation of Relationships for Limited Dependent Variables," *Econometrica* 26 (January 1958), 24–36.

John F. Macdonald and Robert A. Moffitt, "The Uses of Tobit Analysis," *The Review of Economics and Statistics* 62 (May 1980), 318–21, point out that Tobit coefficient estimates do not accurately measure the change in the expected dependent variable (affair in this chapter) except for observations far above the zero limit. The numbers used in the last section in Chapter 5 are thus only approximate.

Chapter 6

As noted in the text, this chapter is taken from an article by Orley Ashenfelter, David Ashmore, and Robert Lalonde, "Bordeaux Wine Vintage Quality and the Weather," *Chance*, 1995, 7–14. The authors supplied me with the data, and I duplicated their results. The 2001 wine prices were supplied by Mt. Carmel Wine, Hamden, Connecticut.

Chapter 7

As noted in the text, this chapter is taken from an article by Garey C. Durden and Larry V. Ellis, "The Effects of Attendance on Student Learning in Principles of Economics," *American Economic Review* 85 (May 1995), 343–46. Box 7-2 is taken from their table 2.

Chapter 8

The material in this chapter is taken from Ray C. Fair, "How Fast Do Old Men Slow Down?" *The Review of Economics and Statistics* 76 (February 1994), 103–18, and an unpublished update. The estimation method used is a combination of the polynomial-spline method and the frontier-function method. This is the most enjoyable paper I have ever written.

Chapter 9

The first example of an estimated interest rate rule is in William G. Dewald and Harry G. Johnson, "An Objective Analysis of the Objectives of American Monetary Policy, 1952–61," in *Banking and Monetary Studies,* ed. Deane Carson (Homewood, Ill.: Richard D. Irwin, 1963), 171–89. I first used an estimated rule in my U.S. macroeconometric model in Ray C. Fair, "The Sensitivity of Fiscal Policy Effects to Assumptions About the Behavior of the Federal Reserve," *Econometrica* 46 (September 1978), 1165–79. These rules are sometimes referred to as Taylor rules, named after Professor John Taylor at Stanford. Taylor discusses interest rate rules in John B. Taylor, "Discretion Versus Policy Rules in Practice," *Carnegie-Rochester Series on Public Policy* 39 (1993), 195–214. These rules should probably be called Dewald-Johnson rules, since Dewald and Johnson preceded Taylor by about 30 years. The estimates in this chapter are taken from Ray C. Fair, "Actual Federal Reserve Policy Behavior and Interest Rate Rules," *FRBNY Economic Policy Review* (March 2001), 61–72. The estimation method used is two stage least squares.

Chapter 10

The price equation in this chapter is taken from my U.S. macroeconometric model. The equation dated January 29, 2000, is used for the estimates. See my Web site: http://fairmodel.econ.yale.edu. The estimation method used is two stage least squares.

Glossary

- **after-the-fact prediction**—A prediction made using the actual values of all the explanatory variables. This is the relevant prediction for testing a theory.
- **coefficient**—A number, such as the value of a slope. A set of coefficients is determined by finding the set that leads to the smallest sum of squared errors.
- **data mining**—The process of trying many explanatory variables and choosing those that lead to the best fit. Doing this increases the chances that the results are a fluke.
- **dependent variable**—The variable explained by the theory.
- **explanatory variable**—A variable that the theory says affects the dependent variable. Also known as *independent variable*.
- **horse race**—The process of including two or more competing explanatory variables in the analysis to see if one is significant and the others are not.
- **independent variable**—*See* **explanatory variable.**
- **omitted variable bias**—An estimated coefficient for an explanatory variable that is biased because some other explanatory variable has been omitted that truly affects the dependent variable and that is also related to the explanatory variable.
- **other things being equal**—Holding everything else the same. Nothing changes except the one thing being considered at the time.
- **real-time prediction**—A prediction made before all the actual values of the explanatory variables are known.

- **selection bias**—Bias that occurs when the probability that a person will answer a survey depends on the size of the dependent variable.
- **significant**—A coefficient value is significant if the probability is small that one would get that value if the true coefficient were zero. We are using a cutoff probability of about 5 percent in this book, which is conventional.
- **standard error of the line**—A measure of the size of a typical error.
- **standard error of the estimated slope**—A measure of the size of a typical error that is made determining a slope.
- *t*-**statistic**—The ratio of a coefficient value to its standard error (the standard error of the estimated slope for that coefficient). A *t*-statistic greater than 2.0 or less than −2.0 means it is very unlikely that the true value of the coefficient is zero.
- **variable**—Something that varies, like across time or across people.

Poetry Credits

Introduction

From SELECTED POEMS, NEW EDITION by W. H. Auden, edited by Edward Mendelson, copyright © 1979 by Edward Mendelson, William Meredith, and Monroe K. Spears, executors of the Estate of W. H. Auden. Preface copyright © 1979 by Edward Mendelson. Used by permission of Vintage Books, a division of Random House, Inc.

Chapter 2

Cunningham, J. V. *The Poems of J. V. Cunningham,* Swallow Press/Ohio University Press, 1997. Reprinted with permission from publisher.

Chapter 3

Reprinted with the permission of Scribner, a Division of Simon & Schuster, Inc., from THE COLLECTED WORKS OF W. B. YEATS, VOLUME 1: THE POEMS, REVISED, edited by Richard J. Finneran. Copyright © 1940 by Georgie Yeats; copyright renewed © 1968 by Bertha Georgie Yeats, Michael Butler Yeats, and Anne Yeats.

Chapter 7

"The Student" from *Kings, Lords, & Commons: Irish Poems from the Seventh Century to the Nineteenth,* translated by Frank O'Connor (New York: Alfred A. Knopf, 1959). Reprinted with the permission of Joan Daves Agency/Writer's House, Inc., New York, on behalf of the proprietors.

Chapter 8

By Dylan Thomas, from THE POEMS OF DYLAN THOMAS, copyright © 1952 by Dylan Thomas. Reprinted by permission of New Directions Publishing Corp.

Chapter 9

Copyright © 1938 by Ogden Nash, Renewed. Reprinted by permission of Curtis Brown, Ltd.

Index